LIPSMACKIN'
CAR CAMPIN'

LIPSMACKIN' CAR CAMPIN'

Easy and Delicious Recipes for Campground Cooking

CHRISTINE AND TIM CONNERS

FALCONGUIDES

GUILFORD, CONNECTICUT
HELENA, MONTANA

AN IMPRINT OF GLOBE PEQUOT PRESS

FALCONGUIDES®

FalconGuides is an imprint of Globe Pequot Press.

Falcon, FalconGuides, and Outfit Your Mind are registered trademarks of Morris Book Publishing, LLC.

All interior photos by Christine and Tim Conners unless otherwise noted.

Project Editor: David Legere

Design: Sheryl Kober

Layout Artist: Maggie Peterson

Library of Congress Cataloging-in-Publication Data is available on file.

ISBN 978-0-7627-8133-1

Printed in the United States of America

10 9 8 7 6 5 4 3 2 1

To Ken Harbison, long-distance friend of many years, whose passion for cooking and love of the outdoors have combined to make for us a most remarkable mentor.

He makes grass grow for the cattle, and plants for people to cultivate—bringing forth food from the earth: wine that gladdens human hearts, oil to make their faces shine, and bread that sustains their hearts.

PSALMS 104:14-15 (NIV)

CONTENTS

ACKNOWLEDGMENTS

We've had the opportunity to broaden and hone our outdoor cooking skills over the years through our involvement with Scouting, where it is well-known that there is no shortage of great food and creative chefs. Through our work on the Scout's Cookbook series, we've made hundreds of contacts, many of whom have provided much of the raw material that allowed us to pursue a new camp cookbook for the general market.

So to our friends and acquaintances—our wonderful contributors— we remain indebted in gratitude. Without you this book would not have been possible.

An experienced outdoorsman and enormously skilled chef, Ken Harbison has been assisting with our book projects for over ten years now. Once again he lent his talents to the current effort, thoroughly testing and reviewing many of the recipes and concepts. Thanks to you, Ken, our outdoor recipe tester extraordinaire.

And to the fine folks at Globe Pequot Press and FalconGuides, especially Max Phelps and John Burbidge: You patiently entertained our crazy ideas over the years and offered many delightful ones yourselves, including expanding the Lipsmackin' series into new arenas such as this. We've been together for a long time now, and for good reason: You take care of your authors. Thank you.

INTRODUCTION

It's amazing that there aren't more books written about the social dynamics, oddities, and just plain eclectic demography found in the typical campground setting. Fiction or nonfiction, at least a few best sellers are begging to be penned on the subject. After all, where else can one find, dwelling in such proximity, the haves and have-nots, enthusiastic revelers and introspective nature seekers, retired empty nesters and young families with many little ones, a spectrum of nationality and color, and experienced campers and those apprehensive about sleeping on the ground for the first time?

It's a remarkable concept, that such a wide range of classes, ethnicities, personalities, and experiences routinely come together peaceably in this place called the campground. And, despite the effort required to pack a lot of gear in the car, pop-up, or RV just to relocate to a temporary abode, often not even that far from home, a huge number of people around the world happily do so on a regular basis. They clearly love it, but why?

The study of the psychology of the campground could probably produce many doctoral dissertations. But the most obvious glue that ties all campers together is a simple fondness for being outdoors. The answer to the question *Why?*, then, may be no more complicated than that. We spend so much of our lives cocooned in heavily insulated homes or buried deep within office buildings that, after awhile, we yearn to put thinner walls, or none at all, between ourselves and the world outside.

Slowly wander the byways of a campground on any pleasant evening and soak in the festive atmosphere mingled with the aroma of wood smoke. The echo of happy children can be heard from all directions. People, usually too harried to crack a smirk, laugh with gusto. Catch the attention of folks relaxing in their camp chairs, and you're sure to receive a friendly wave in return. The campground is a special place, beyond the natural beauty. Those who frequent it are well acquainted with the feeling.

It is in this spirit that our book is written. Good food may not always make the occasion, but it definitely enhances it. And while there are many things less pleasant than cold sandwiches and plain cereal, possessing the skills, tools, and recipes to produce culinary masterpieces under the open sky will create truly unforgettable memories.

May this book help you do just that. And may new and wonderfully enticing aromas be found drifting from your campsite, drawing in your fellow campers to the special friendship and camaraderie that can only be found outdoors.

Christine and Tim Conners
Statesboro, Georgia

Planning and Preparing Your Meals

The campground is often an educational stepping-stone to the more remote trails and deeper wilderness frequented by hikers and backpackers. In the forgiving environment found close to one's vehicle, many campers learn to become comfortable with wild fauna, unpredictable weather, and occasional planning gaffes without having to endure the same level of consequence that such situations would bring in wild locales far from the car.

As campers planning for the basic needs of food and shelter, we tend to get the shelter part right. But for food, we often bring along options of convenience better aligned with picnics in the park: coolers packed with ho-hum sandwiches, bland tubs of store-bought pasta salad, cans of sugary soda, and a lot of snack and junk foods. These options certainly work in the campground setting and do the job of filling stomachs. But they hardly give justice to the culinary dynamic range that's easily possible in the outdoor kitchen and especially while car camping. Along with more traditional fare from the grill, how about some great grub from the camp stove, Dutch oven, or embers of the fire itself?

In our book, *Lipsmackin' Backpackin',* six attributes critical to excellent trail cuisine are covered in detail: weight, nutritional value, taste, variety, simplicity, and durability. When car camping, weight (and volume) of cooking gear is obviously no longer a factor, nutritional value becomes more aligned with personal needs and preference, and durability can be easily addressed with a large sturdy cooler filled with ice. So the car and cooler uncomplicate the problem of camp menu planning to one that needs to only consider the remaining three attributes: taste, variety, and simplicity.

It is on these three attributes that *Lipsmackin' Car Campin'* places emphasis by presenting great-tasting recipes that are easily and predictably prepared in the campground setting. Our formula for designing this book remains unchanged from the other titles in the *Lipsmackin'* series: Keep the focus on a wide range of tasty, dependable, and simple dishes, then mix in a little fun whenever possible!

Lipsmackin' Car Campin' is a collection of favorite recipes and tips from some of the world's most experienced campers. Recipes have been selected and arranged to maximize the efficiency of the meal-planning process and to steer campers around the usual pitfalls of outdoor cookery. Information is plainly presented to allow the reader to quickly judge the merits of a particular recipe while preparing for a camping trip. And each recipe is clearly structured for foolproof preparation once in the outdoors. Expansive instructional material in the front matter, along with resource and reference lists in the back, make the book all the more useful in planning and preparing for your next camping excursion.

The following section, along with the remaining portions of this chapter, explain the general layout of *Lipsmackin' Car Campin'* and how the information presented can specifically assist with camp meal planning and preparation.

Recipe Categories

There are as many ways to organize a cookbook as there are eating styles and preferences. The approach that appears to satisfy most people, and the one used in this book, is to begin by organizing entrees according to the meal category they best belong to: breakfast, lunch, or dinner. Those recipes that could not readily be tagged as "main dish" were grouped into four other primary categories: side dishes, breads, snacks and desserts, and drinks.

A special note is warranted regarding the lunch section, which was constructed around the premise that campers are either on the move at midday or kicking back, siesta style—neither situation making a challenging menu attractive. And so noontime meals have been selected based on ease of preparation and cleanup. Only those recipes with an estimated total preparation time of an hour or less were included in the lunch category. Many of the lunch recipes also call for a campfire as the heat source, with the premise that the early campfire will have died down by late morning to produce a gentle bed of embers perfect for cooking. Of course if you want to prepare a more involved meal at midday, consult the recipes in the dinner section, many of which perform equally well at the noon hour.

Servings

For consistency, serving estimates assume the target audience to be active adults on a moderate caloric intake. Serving sizes were adjusted upward as credit for healthier recipes and downward for those with less desirable nutrition characteristics. Adjust your estimates according to your specific situation, keeping in mind that activity level, richness of the meal, food preferences, snacking, weather, and altitude will all influence the actual number of servings you'll obtain from each recipe.

Many established campgrounds impose a strict limit to the number of campers at each site, and the recipes take this into consideration: The maximum number of servings found in this book rarely exceeds six to eight and never exceeds eight to ten. However, it's a straightforward task to multiply recipes to meet the needs of larger groups. If more servings are desired, you can scale up many of the recipes by simply replicating the dish as required. This is a fairly obvious approach that doesn't require further explanation.

But some recipes do permit a significant increase (or decrease) in the number of servings using the original equipment specified in the recipe. For instance, a recipe that calls for a cook pot that produces half a dozen servings might be able to squeeze in several more just by adding more ingredients to the pot.

Challenge Level

A three-tier system has been used to assign a challenge level to each recipe: "easy," "moderate," or "difficult." The decision was based on the preparation and cleanup effort required in camp, the sensitivity of the cooking technique to variation, and the attention to care necessary to avoid injury. Most of the recipes in this book have been tagged as "easy," an important quality especially for the camp setting, where simplicity is definitely welcome.

Preparation Time

Total preparation time under pleasant weather conditions has been esti-mated for each recipe. Rounded to the nearest quarter hour, this value includes the time required to prepare the heat source (if required) through to serving the dish. It is assumed that the chef will flow the preparation steps in parallel and use assistance whenever possible. For instance, while the coals are starting or water is being brought to a boil, other prepa-ration steps can often be accomplished simultaneously. The recipes are written to best take advantage of this.

Preparation Instructions

Instructions for each recipe include a list of ingredients, carefully selected to create less waste of key items. Also included are step-by-step direc-tions, each logically grouped and presented in numerical sequence. The use of numerical sequencing in the preparation steps is intended to help you stay focused and to assist in the assignment of specific tasks to other campers able to lend a hand. This is especially important for larger groups, where the delegation of tasks is an important component to smooth and successful meal preparation. The recipes in this book are prepared completely in camp, none requiring at-home preparation steps in advance.

Heating instructions are clear and consistent and provide high probability of success under a wide range of cooking conditions. For extra precision with Dutch oven recipes, an exact number of standard-size briquettes (coals) is specified for use on the lid and under the oven.

If an actual baking temperature is required, say, to modify a Dutch oven recipe or to adapt it to a larger or smaller oven, use the conversion chart below to make the transformation by converting the specified coal count and Dutch oven size back into a temperature value. This conversion chart, based on data from Lodge Manufacturing, is very reliable when cooking with cast-iron stoves under pleasant weather conditions and using standard-size, high-quality briquettes, fresh from the charcoal starter.

Coal-Temperature Conversion Chart

Dutch Oven Diameter		Oven Temperature					
		325°F	350°F	375°F	400°F	425°F	450°F
8"	Total Briquettes	15	16	17	18	19	20
	On Lid	10	11	11	12	13	14
	Underneath Oven	5	5	6	6	6	6
10"	Total Briquettes	19	21	23	25	27	29
	On Lid	13	14	16	17	18	19
	Underneath Oven	6	7	7	8	9	10
12"	Total Briquettes	23	25	27	29	31	33
	On Lid	16	17	18	19	21	22
	Underneath Oven	7	8	9	10	10	11
14"	Total Briquettes	30	32	34	36	38	40
	On Lid	20	21	22	24	25	26
	Underneath Oven	10	11	12	12	13	14
16"	Total Briquettes	37	39	41	43	45	47
	On Lid	25	26	27	28	29	30
	Underneath Oven	12	13	14	15	16	17

Options and Tips

Interesting cooking options are provided for many of the recipes. Options differ from the main instructions and produce alternate endings to the recipe. Options included with a recipe are shown separately from the main preparation steps.

Likewise, contributors occasionally offer helpful tips that can assist the camp chef with purchasing ingredients or preparing the recipe in some way. As with options, tips are listed separately from the main body of the recipe. Recommendations and tips of a more generic nature, or applicable to a wider range of recipes and situations, are grouped separately.

Equipment Requirements

A list of cooking equipment required at camp follows each set of instructions. For reasons of practicality, not every item required to prepare a recipe is listed. For example, a cooler or refrigeration device is obviously essential for keeping perishable foods safe. It is assumed that one is always available for use. Other gear assumed to be basic equipment residing in any camp kitchen includes the following:

- Food thermometer
- Measuring cups and spoons
- Can opener
- Cutting and paring knives
- Cutting boards
- Long-handled wooden spoons
- Long-handled ladle
- A food-grade greasing agent, such as vegetable oil
- Serving plates, utensils, cups, and napkins
- Wash basins, scrub pads, dish detergent, and towels
- Hand sanitizer
- Work tables and serving tables
- Heavy barbecue gloves

It is also assumed that you have the necessary tools and equipment available for preparing and managing the heat source required for each selected recipe, such as briquettes, coal starter, coal tray, tongs, and lid lifter when using a camp Dutch oven. When a recipe's equipment necessities go beyond the list of these basics, those requirements are listed with each recipe to head off any surprises in camp.

When bowls, skillets, or cooking pots are specified for some recipes, "small," "medium-size," and "large" are used to approximate the capacity to do the job. By having several sizes of utensils available at camp, you'll never find yourself in a pickle during food preparation. If ever in doubt on utensil size requirements, err on the side of larger capacity.

More information on camp Dutch ovens can be found in later sections of the book, but you'll only need a few sizes to prepare any Dutch oven recipe in this book. A 10-inch/4-quart oven, adequate for most cooking tasks, is specified for the majority of Dutch oven recipes. This size is perfect for producing six to eight servings and is perhaps the most versatile oven to purchase for car camping if you currently don't own one. On rare occasions, a 12-inch/6-quart or deep 14-inch/10-quart is called for because the larger internal volume is necessary for some roasting and baking jobs. And a couple of recipes call for an 8-inch/2-quart oven, great for rich desserts or a smaller number of servings. Camp Dutch ovens of sizes other than these are also available; while these can be handy when adapting a dish for a different number of servings, they are not required to use this book.

Some recipes call for the use of a gadget known as a pie iron, the camp version of the kitchen panini press. Made from cast iron and situated on the end of a long handle, pie irons are simple devices designed to toast stuffed sandwiches and shell-based filled desserts directly in or over the campfire. If you've never heard of such a thing, no worries. You'll find them easy to use and a lot of fun.

Contributor Information
Rounding out each recipe is information about the contributors. These are the field experts who made the book possible. You'll learn their names and the places of residence they call home. Many of our contributors included anecdotes and stories as well. Useful and often humorous, you'll find these before each recipe.

Category System

This book uses a category system that allows you to rapidly assess the most appropriate recipe options when planning a menu for the campground. Five key considerations are typically used when developing a list of candidate recipes: 1) the equipment available, 2) the number of people to prepare for, 3) the time available to prepare the meal, 4) the level of skill required to achieve good results, and 5) any special nutrition requirements.

To help ensure you pack the proper gear along with the food, the required cooking method necessary *in camp*—Dutch oven, cook pot, frying pan, campfire, grill, or no cook—is indicated by corresponding icons. You want a firm idea of the number of servings each recipe will produce so that the recipe can be scaled, if necessary. Serving numbers, usually expressed as a range, are given for this purpose. Preparation time is also provided and rounded to the nearest quarter hour. Simplicity is addressed through the challenge level assigned to each recipe—"easy," "moderate," or "difficult."

For campers looking specifically for meatless options, a **V-LO** icon is used to identify the recipe as lacto-ovo vegetarian, free of meat but containing dairy and/or egg products. For recipes free of not only meat but also dairy and egg, an icon simply indicating **V** marks the selection as vegan.

As discussed earlier in this section, recipes are first grouped at top level by meal category, forming the core chapters of the book. But from there, the recipes have been subgrouped by the required cooking method, then by the number of servings, followed by the preparation time, and, finally, by the challenge level. Number of servings, preparation time, and challenge level are listed prominently at the start of each recipe, specifically addressing several of the key considerations already discussed.

The icon system that identifies the required cooking method, and is located at the top of each recipe, is defined in the following table.

With one glance the icon system provides a rapid introduction to the primary tools and heat sources required for each recipe. Using the icon system, you can move quickly past the recipes that aren't an option. No simple system can perfectly categorize every recipe. For example, some recipes may call for the use of a cook pot and a Dutch oven. In cases like these, where more than one icon was an option, we identified the recipe by the technique most critical to the recipe's success.

Recipe Icons Category System

	Dutch oven with coals
	Cook pot on camp stove
	Skillet on camp stove or fire
	Foil, pie iron, or skewer over flames or in fire pit
	Foil, skewer, or other direct heating on grill
	No heat source required

Supplemental Information for the Camp Chef

Additional information is included in the front and back sections of the book to assist with the challenge of outdoor cooking. An important section on safety (below) highlights the most common risks found in the camp kitchen and what can be done to help reduce the probability of an accident. Be safe. Review this material, especially if you are new to camp cooking.

Hand in hand with safety comes skill. An expert camp cook is far less likely to inflict injury or illness to either him- or herself or fellow campers. A section on basic skills (later in this chapter) reviews the competencies that outdoor cooks should seek to understand and master.

The appendices cover a wide variety of helpful reference information, including kitchen measurement conversions, sources of camp cooking gear and ingredients, a bibliography of additional books and information on outdoor cooking, and techniques for reducing the environmental impact of camp cooking.

Healthy Pairings

Wise choices and moderation are the keys to maintaining a healthy diet in camp, and these begin with the planning process. When choosing recipes that lean toward higher fats and sugars, balance your meals with light salads or fresh vegetables. Instead of pairing a heavy entree with a rich dessert, select a lighter after-dinner option, such as fresh fruit. If everyone's favorite decadent dessert is on the menu, choose a less rich dinner to go with it. Avoid serving multiple courses at a meal, which not only complicates meal planning and cleanup but also contributes to overeating.

Between meals, have plenty of healthy snacks available instead of fatty and sugary cookies and candy. Bananas, oranges, clementines, peaches, nectarines, plums, apples, and carrots are all easy to store and serve while in camp. In-shell peanuts and tortilla chips and salsa make for favorite between-meal snacks.

Camp Cooking Safety

The outdoor kitchen presents some of the more significant hazards that a camper will face, and yet the risks are often taken for granted. Most people have learned to successfully manage dangers in the home kitchen through caution and experience. But *camp* cooking presents many new and unique hazards that, if not appreciated and controlled, can cause severe injury or illness. The following information on cooking safety highlights the most common risks found in the camp kitchen and what can be done to help reduce the probability of an accident.

While the goal should always be zero accidents, minor injuries, including cuts and burns, are not uncommon. Keep the first-aid kit handy for these. Never acceptable, however, are more serious injuries or food-borne illness. Extreme care and caution should always be used to prevent accidents that could otherwise send you or your diners to the doctor or hospital.

Be careful. Searing hot metal can char your skin instantly. Sharp knifes can go deep into your body before your brain has time to register what is happening. Heavy cast iron dropped on your foot can smash unprotected bones. Harmful bacteria left alive due to improper cooking can leave you so ill that your body barely clings to life.

Learn to respect *every* step of the cooking process. Always think about what you are about to do and ask yourself, "Is this safe?" If it isn't, or even if you are uncomfortable for reasons you don't understand, trust your instinct. Stop and determine how to do the job better, either by using more appropriate techniques and equipment or by asking others for assistance or advice.

And don't try to mimic the chefs you see on TV. That fancy speed chopping might look impressive, but it's dangerous if you don't know what you're doing. Move slowly and methodically. No matter how hungry your crew may be, no meal is worth compromising health and well-being.

With care and attention, any cooking risk can be managed to an acceptable level. The following list of guidelines for safety will help you do just that.

Supervision and Assistance

- First and foremost, a responsible adult must always carefully supervise the cooking activities of inexperienced adults or children, even more so when heat, sharp utensils, or raw meat is involved.

- The picnic table, ubiquitous in most campground settings, often serves as a useful surface for many functions: cooking, serving, dining, and cleaning being the most obvious. But because the picnic table is already the center of such a busy area, it's best to move the cooking to a less chaotic part of camp to avoid unnecessary distraction or interference.

- When setting up your camp kitchen, structure the preparation area according to work flow to minimize the chances of your assistants running into either you or each other, especially when carrying sharp knives, hot food, or heavy equipment. Give everyone plenty of room to work.

- When cooking for larger groups, the workload will increase, as will the probability of falling behind schedule. If you find yourself trailing, don't rush to catch up. The chances of accident and injury will only increase. And don't be a martyr, suffering silently under the burden. You'll only fatigue yourself all the more quickly. Instead, immediately enlist help from other skilled members of your group to help get the meal preparation back on track.

Food Poisoning

- Ensure that recipes containing raw meat or eggs are thoroughly cooked. Use a food thermometer to take several readings at various locations throughout the food being prepared. Minimum safe cooking temperatures vary by food type, but 165°F is high enough to kill all common food-borne pathogens. Use this value when in doubt.

- Cold and wet weather can significantly lower the temperature of the heat source and cookware. To compensate, prepare to increase the length of cooking time, or, if using a Dutch oven, the number of coals. Windy weather can have an unpredictable effect on a Dutch oven, the temperature within the oven sometimes becoming uneven. The use of a food thermometer is especially recommended in all cases of adverse weather when cooking raw meat or eggs.

- Care should be taken when handling raw meat or eggs to prevent cross-contamination of other foods such as raw vegetables. When preparing raw meats, cutting surfaces and utensils should be dedicated *only* to this task or thoroughly washed with detergent prior to use for other purposes. Avoid the mistake of placing just-cooked food into an unwashed bowl or tray used earlier to mix or hold raw meats or eggs.

- In the potential confusion of a larger group setting, with several assistants working together in the camp kitchen, it is important to clearly communicate to the others if work surfaces or utensils are being used to prepare raw meat or eggs. Otherwise the equipment may be used improperly by others, leading to cross-contamination of the food.

- Raw meat and eggs should be tightly sealed in a container or ziplock bag and placed in a cooler until ready to use. To avoid cross-contamination, keep these items in their own cooler, separate from drinking ice, raw fruits, vegetables, cheese, beverages, or any other items that will not eventually be cooked at high temperature.

- Drinking ice must be stored in its own clean and dedicated cooler. Ice from a cooler used for storing raw meats and eggs should never be used in beverages.

- Sanitize your work area, and hands, with antibacterial cleaners appropriate for the kitchen both before and after the meal.

- Using soap and water or hand sanitizer, thoroughly clean your hands *immediately* after you've handled raw meat or eggs and *before* touching any other cooking instruments or ingredients. If you must repeatedly touch raw meat or eggs during preparation, then repeatedly sanitize your hands before handling anything else. Be sure that you and the rest of the kitchen crew are compulsive about this. It's that important.

- All food that could potentially spoil, including leftovers, should be kept on ice. To prolong the life of your ice, store coolers in a shady, cool, secure location, with lids tightly sealed. Covering the coolers with sleeping bags or blankets on a warm day will further insulate them.

- Be sure that water used for cooking has been properly treated or purified before using. Do not simply assume that any water from a camp spigot is safe to drink. Ask camp officials if you are unsure.

Cuts, Burns, and Broken Bones

- Cutting utensils are inherently dangerous, and it goes without saying that they should be handled with care. Dull blades can be more dangerous than sharper instruments. Dull knife blades unintentionally slip much more easily when slicing or chopping and can quickly end up in the side of your finger instead of the food you're cutting. Maintaining the sharpness of knife blades will help ensure they do what you expect. When slicing and chopping, always keep hands and fingers from the underside of the cutting edge or from in front of the blade tip.

- Do not share a cutting board concurrently with one of your kitchen colleagues. You could end up injuring each other. Instead, take turns using the board, or employ a second one for use.

- Extreme care should be taken when cleaning and storing sharp kitchen instruments. A knife at the bottom of a washbasin filled with cloudy water is a potential booby trap for the unlucky dishwasher who doesn't know it's there. Don't leave knives hidden in soapy water. The same holds true when storing sharp utensils after cleaning. Knives, in particular, should be sheathed in a holder when placed back in storage.

- When using a cookstove to prepare food in a pot or frying pan, be sure that long handles, if any, are turned away from the edge of the stove or table to prevent inadvertently knocking or spilling the hot contents onto your skin.

- Do not use a cook pot or frying pan that is too large for the cookstove. If a pot or pan significantly overhangs the burner grill, it could topple. If your setup is unstable, switch to a smaller pot or pan, or find a larger stove.

- Never use a flimsy table for cooking. It could buckle under the weight and send the hot stove and food flying. Any table used for cooking must be sturdy.

- Use protective gear, such as heavy leather barbecue gloves, on both hands when handling hot coals or tending a cooking fire. Ensure that the gloves are long enough to protect your forearms. If you fail to regularly use heavy protective gloves in these situations, you are likely to eventually suffer a nasty burn. Closed-top shoes are also required. The top of your bare foot won't quickly forget a red-hot briquette landing snugly between your sandal straps.

- Cast-iron cookware is heavy. But a large Dutch oven or frying pan filled to the brim with hot food is *extremely* heavy . . . and dangerous. Wear heatproof gloves and closed-top footwear when handling hot and loaded cast iron. And if the cookware is too heavy for you to safely manage alone, swallow your pride and ask for help.

- Cast iron retains heat for a long time after it is removed from the coals. This is a great quality for keeping food warm during mealtime, but it also sets the stage for burn injuries to the unsuspecting. Before moving any cast iron with unprotected hands after the meal, carefully check to be sure the metal has cooled sufficiently. If it hasn't, or if you're unsure, use heatproof gloves.

Fire Safety

- All cooking must be performed in a fire-safe area of camp, clear of natural combustibles like dry leaves, grass, and trees, and away from wooden structures. When cooking directly on the ground using coals, select a durable area covered in fireproof material such as rock, gravel, or bare earth. Be sure to follow any special open-fire restrictions established for your region. If unsure, ask camp officials about this when checking in. Always have a large bucket of water handy to douse any flames that may escape your fire-safe perimeter.

- When using a cookstove, keep loose and combustible items such as dish towels, plastic bags, aprons, long sleeves, shirts, and hair away from the flame.

- Cooking fires require special attention to avoid injury. Keep the fire just large enough to do the job. Use long-handled tongs when managing foods in the fire. If cooking above a fire using a grill grate, ensure that the grate is strong and sturdy enough to handle the weight of the cookware and food that you're placing on it. Be sure the fire is cold out before leaving camp.

- Hot coals on the ground present a potential hazard during cooking, but especially afterward. With a Dutch oven off the heat, and with the coals ashed over, the threat lurking in your cooking area might go unnoticed. Notify your fellow campers of the danger of hot coals on the ground. Keep the area off-limits to all but essential personnel until the coals expire. Once the coals have fully cooled, discard the ash in a fire-safe manner appropriate for your camp.

- Unless vented, noxious fumes from a camp stove or burning coals will rise and concentrate within the apex of any roof under which cooking is performed. So when a kitchen tent or tarp structure is used for cooking in camp, the apex must be substantially higher than a tall person's head, and with walls open and well ventilated on all sides. When cooking in a kitchen tent, be especially diligent to maintain a large fire-safe perimeter around the cooking area. Never attempt to cook in a *sleeping* tent. The fully enclosed walls will concentrate deadly gases and cause asphyxiation; or the tent floor or walls could rapidly catch fire and trap the occupants. A standard picnic canopy with low ceiling or partially enclosed side walls is also unsafe for cooking because the apex is at head height and the walls are often too low or poorly ventilated.

- Do not use a barbecue grill in a kitchen tent. A flare-up could create a fire hazard, and any concentration of smoke could be dangerous.

Allergies and Special Diets

When planning a menu for a group outing, be sure to consider food allergies or health issues that might require special dietary restrictions. Selecting recipes that meet everyone's tastes and requirements may seem impossible in these circumstances, but many recipes can be modified to meet dietary requirements while satisfying everyone else in the group. This approach can be far easier than attempting to adhere to a parallel special-requirements menu.

Wild Animals

Animals searching for food scraps and garbage can pose a danger to the camp environment, either through aggression or disease. Unattended dirty dishes, unsecured garbage, food items and coolers left in the open—all of these will eventually attract unwanted animal attention and can create a major problem, especially in bear country. Wildlife that gains access to such goodies will surely come back for more, placing these animals at risk of harm along with the people who must then interact with them or remove them. A camp kept neat and clean, with food and garbage properly stored and secured, is far less attractive to the local fauna. Practice low-impact camping principles and adhere to any food storage regulations unique to your area or camp.

No list can cover every potential danger, and this is surely no exception. But by learning to cook with a mind fixated on safety, few circumstances will catch you ill prepared or by surprise.

Basic Skills for the Camp Chef

Good camp cooking isn't magical, nor does it come by accident. A strong foundation in the fundamentals of outdoor cookery will make it all the more likely you'll be successful. With this in mind, the following section covers the essential skills.

Planning for the Obvious . . . and the Unexpected

- If you are a camp-cooking neophyte, keep your menu simple, especially when preparing food for larger crowds. Raise the challenge level only after becoming more skilled and confident in your abilities. Taking on more work than one can manage is a common camp-kitchen mistake, and the botched meal that results is sure to disappoint not only the one doing the work but any hungry stomachs depending on the chef.

- Many recipes serve admirably as "one-pot" meals. These are perfect for newer chefs, where simplicity is welcome. Unless you are looking for a real challenge, avoid complex, multipot meals and rely instead on a one-pot entree and a simple side or two, such as fresh salad and sliced bread. Aluminum "steam table pans" make excellent and inexpensive containers for serving large quantities of salads and breads to large groups.

- Once the gear is purchased, groceries account for the majority of cost on many outings. However, now is not the time to be overly frugal. Cost cutting can be taken to an extreme, with ingredients of such low quality that it's painfully obvious, meal after meal. Consider spending the additional money on quality ingredients. You'll appreciate the difference once at camp.

- The ability to multitask is a hallmark of great chefs, and it becomes even more important when dealing with large quantities of ingredients or when replicating recipes. Don't act as the Lone Ranger when cooking for large groups. Enlist help and divide kitchen duties to lighten the load while cooking and cleaning. Discuss roles and responsibilities in advance so there is no confusion when it comes time to engage. The recipes in this book use numerical sequencing for the instructions. Use these to best assign tasks to the helpers.

- They are often enthusiastic to assist, but inexperienced adults and younger children require more supervision. Make sure you can manage the additional workload when assigning tasks to the tenderfoots. Some don't know a can opener from a pizza cutter or won't have a clue as to how to crack an egg. If cooking under trying circumstances, it may be better to leave the inexperienced chefs out of the kitchen altogether.

- The younger the children, the more they tend to openly grumble about their food, even when it is obviously awesome to everyone else. And after a long evening of cooking in camp, complaining is the last thing you want to hear. A powerful way to avoid this is to include all of your fellow campers, especially the younger ones, in the meal-planning process. By giving them a voice, they become stakeholders in the meal's success and are more likely to enjoy the results.

- Read through and understand the *entire* recipe before commencing preparation. You are far less likely to make a critical mistake by doing so. And be sure to have everything you need before starting a recipe by first gathering all ingredients and cooking utensils to your work area.

- When planning your menu, don't ignore the flexibility of the camp Dutch oven, which can be used in place of a frying pan, grill grate, or cook pot for many recipes that otherwise require one. If a camp stove, barbecue grill, or wood fire will be unavailable for your favorite recipes at your next outing, consider adapting these dishes to the circumstances. A camp Dutch oven and a bag of briquettes can probably do the job easily and admirably.

- Foul weather adds a powerful variable to the camp cooking equation. And bugs and wild animals further distract by keeping the cook on the defensive. Prior to any outing, weather and critters should be considered and planned for appropriately. Be realistic about what you can handle under the circumstances likely to be encountered. The more trying the conditions, the simpler the menu should be.

- Even the most foolproof dish sometimes ends its short life tragically dumped in the dirt by fate or accident. Whatever the cause may be, always have a Plan B at the ready, whether boxed macaroni or a map to the nearest grocery store. At some point you are likely to need it.

Tailoring Your Camp Kitchen

- Once arriving at camp, give careful thought to your kitchen area. Set up the work tables in a quiet, level corner, if possible. Choose an area with a durable surface. Otherwise all the foot traffic will wear down grasses and sensitive plant growth. Avoid muddy or low-lying areas, especially if rain is in the forecast. The kitchen must be in a fire-safe area. If using a campfire or Dutch oven, the cooking area should be adjacent to the camp kitchen so that a close eye can be kept on the situation. When using coals or a campfire, a fire-safe perimeter must be established around the cooking area, free of all combustibles.

- Consider your work flow and logically position the cooking area, work tables, serving tables, storage bins, coolers, and trash containers to minimize cross traffic (and collisions) within the kitchen area. If possible, position the main kitchen away from the serving area so that hungry diners don't get in the way of the chefs as they go about finishing their tasks. In fact, a good option is to use the campground's picnic table for serving, while keeping the kitchen area itself well clear of that busy hot spot.

- Many, but certainly not all, campgrounds provide a barbecue grill in each individual campsite. Before structuring your menu around the presumed presence of a camp grill, confirm with the campground office that one will indeed be available if you are unsure. Bring along a wire brush to clean and scrape the grill's grate before using, and pack your own portable campfire grate as backup in the event that the actual camp grill turns out to be in disrepair or unsafe. Portable grates are inexpensive and easy to find in the camping section at larger retailers.

- When cooking for large groups, bring along extra mixing bowls and other less expensive utensils, such as knives, measuring cups, and long-handled mixing spoons. That way any assistants will never be without the tools needed to do their job. And always have several cutting boards available. Lack of adequate cutting equipment is a common bottleneck in the camp kitchen.

- Have plenty of sturdy folding tables when cooking for large groups. Otherwise, if table space is very limited, and some of the food preparation is relegated out of necessity to the serving area or to the ground, the process can quickly become unhygienic, inefficient, and frustrating. Keep in mind that extra table space will also be required for serving the food.

Reduce, Reuse, Recycle

- Avoid waste by setting out only the number of serving plates, bowls, and utensils required for the meal. Consider asking your campmates to reuse their serving ware for other courses, such as salad or dessert. Have a permanent marker available for writing names on disposable plastic cups so that these can be reused. Better yet, maintain and use your own personal mess kits when camping, or, at the least, bring along durable plastic drinking cups from home with names marked on them.

- Some serving ware, though disposable, is robust enough to pass through the dishwasher. If this is the case for your situation, consider using a bin, box, aluminum steam table pan, or bag to collect used utensils once they've been rinsed. Then clean them in bulk later, in the dishwasher at home, for future reuse.

Managing the Heat

- When using a cook pot, skillet, or Dutch oven on a grate over a campfire, the cooking temperature is much easier to control if the flames are low and the fire has a solid, level bed of embers. If you plan to use open fire as your heat source, start the campfire long before mealtime to give it time to die down and stabilize.

- Foil packets are convenient for cooking many types of foods. But this is one of the more challenging methods for properly controlling temperature and avoiding over- or undercooked foods. When using foil packets, more predictable results can be obtained if the packets are placed on a grate over a campfire, briquettes, or propane grill, as opposed to tossing the foil packets directly onto the embers of a campfire. It's important to use a tight seal to trap moisture, along with a generous air pocket for the contents, because the food cooks, in part, by steaming. Heavy-duty foil is recommended, and if the fire is particularly hot, use two layers, wrapping your food in the first sheet, tightly sealing the edges, then doing the same with the second sheet.

- Select a high-quality briquette of standard size when using charcoal with a Dutch oven. Extra-large or small briquettes, or even embers from the campfire, can also work, but their nonstandard size will make it more challenging to achieve proper results when following a cookbook, such as this one, that specifies exact coal counts based on a standard briquette size.

- Many Dutch oven recipes with a high liquid content, such as stews, can easily tolerate nonexact briquette counts. Because of this, irregular-size coals from the campfire can be readily used as the fuel source instead. By using embers from the campfire, the additional twenty minutes or so otherwise required to start briquettes from scratch is eliminated. Reducing the preparation time in this manner also makes many Dutch oven dinner recipes a viable option at lunchtime, even when the schedule is tight.

- Intense heat is transferred through the walls of a Dutch oven in those areas where coals come into *direct contact* with the metal. Food touching the walls on the inside surface of these hot spots will likely char. With coals usually on the lid by default, it is imperative that tall foods, such as rising breads or roasts, are cooked in a Dutch oven deep enough to keep the food from contacting the lid's inside surface. Below the oven, the briquettes must be positioned to not directly touch the metal's underside, or the food on the floor of the oven will probably burn. If these simple rules are followed, you should never find it necessary to scrape carbon from your breads or expensive cuts of meat.

- Briquettes often clump together when you place or move the oven during cooking. They sometimes congregate on the lid, but their sly gatherings usually occur under the oven, where their unruly behavior is more difficult to observe. The problem is that the clumping can create hot spots that produce uneven cooking, especially while baking. To prevent this, redistribute the wayward coals as necessary, especially under the oven, and rotate the oven one-quarter turn over the briquettes every fifteen minutes or so. At the same time, use a lid lifter to carefully rotate the lid one-quarter turn relative to the base.

- Heat escapes quickly when the lid is raised from a Dutch oven. Tempting as it may be to continually peek at that cheesecake, don't do so unless necessary. You'll only lengthen the cooking time.

- Hot briquettes quickly fail when used directly on moist surfaces. Avoid this common mistake by placing your coals and oven on a metal tray or other durable, dry, fireproof surface, such as the flat side of a row of cinder blocks. A tray or hard surface prevents the oven from settling down into the soil and onto direct contact with the coals under the oven, which could otherwise cause the food to char. Cooking on a tray or raised surface also protects the ground from scarring and makes ash cleanup and disposal easier once the coals expire.

- Always bring plenty of extra charcoal briquettes to cover contingencies. Food preparation may take longer than expected, requiring additional coals to complete the meal. Windy, cold, or wet weather can also greatly increase the number of coals required. Don't get caught with an empty bag of briquettes and half-baked food.

- Preheat the Dutch oven in recipes that require hot metal to properly kick-start the cooking process, such as when sautéing vegetables or browning meats. An exact coal count isn't essential for preheating the oven, with about two dozen briquettes generally adequate for the job. When browning or sautéing, all the coals go under the oven because the lid is unused. When preheating the oven for recipes requiring the lid, the coals should be distributed between the lid and under the oven. Use any unspent coals for subsequent cooking steps.

- Most recipes for the Dutch oven are remarkably resilient against overcooking. The heavy, tight-fitting lid helps trap moisture, which prevents foods from drying out when left on the coals longer than they need to be. However, as is true in the home kitchen, *baked* items require more precision for great results. So pay closer attention to temperature and timing when baking.

- When cooking with more than one Dutch oven at mealtime, stacking the ovens, one on top of the other, can be a useful technique if the cooking area is limited. This method also saves on briquettes, as the coals on the lid of the bottom oven also heat the bottom of the oven on top. But be aware that stacking complicates the preparation, requiring careful placement of the ovens and more attention to coal distribution and cooking times. For instance, you wouldn't want to place a dish that requires frequent stirring at the bottom of the stack. Nor would you stack a Dutch oven that uses a low coal count on top of one requiring a lot of briquettes. Stacking several ovens can also be more hazardous, as a taller tower becomes more prone to toppling. Plan carefully and be extra cautious when using stacks.

Dealing with the Weather

- When a coal-covered Dutch oven lid is lifted while the wind is stirring, or if the lid is bumped while lifting, you'll watch in helpless wonder as ash majestically floats down onto your food. It's a beautiful sight, like powdered sugar on a chocolate cake. Unfortunately, ash doesn't taste like powdered sugar. So avoid jarring the lid when lifting, and remove it immediately toward the downwind side. This will minimize your ash-to-food ratio.

- In very windy conditions place your stove or Dutch oven behind a windscreen of some sort while cooking; otherwise the food will be subjected to uneven heating, potentially burned in some areas and undercooked in others. A row of coolers or storage bins can serve handily as a windbreak. Dutch oven stands, purpose-built for cooking off the ground, often come with built-in windscreens.

- Very chilly or windy weather can present a real challenge to keeping food warm prior to serving. Foods cooked in the Dutch oven can be left inside the oven until served, as the heft of the oven itself is very effective at trapping and holding heat. Cooked foods can also be placed in aluminum steam table trays, covered with foil, then layered in dry dish towels for insulation. A gas grill with a cover is also effective. Even coolers holding a few hot rocks from around the perimeter of the fire can serve as warming ovens, provided the rocks aren't so hot as to melt the plastic.

- Perhaps the most challenging of all outdoor cooking situations in an open kitchen involves rain. In a heavy downpour, the only options may be to cease and desist to wait it out, serve no-cook foods instead, or move the camp kitchen to a fire-safe covered area. Never cook in a sleeping tent.

- When using Dutch ovens in the rain, large sheets of heavy-duty aluminum foil, tented loosely over the top of the oven and tray, can offer some protection in a pinch but are unlikely to shield completely during a cloudburst. A large barbecue grill with a lid can protect your oven from the rain, with a metal tray placed on the grill grate serving as the cook surface. And, once again, a Dutch oven stand with a windscreen would serve nicely, with the screen supporting sheets of heavy foil or a tray for keeping the rain off the coals.

- A camp kitchen tent is arguably the most comfortable option for cooking in wet weather, but good judgment is a must when choosing and using a kitchen tent because of the very real risk of asphyxiation and fire. See the section earlier in this chapter for important information on kitchen tent safety.

- Cooking with a Dutch oven in snow presents it own unique difficulties, but these are easily managed if planned for in advance. If the snow is deep and cannot be easily cleared, cook off the ground on a durable surface. For example, a metal tray on a concrete picnic table works well in this instance. A Dutch oven stand can also be very useful in the snow. If your camping area has a sturdy grill, you can use a tray placed on the grate. You can also arrange wood logs in the snow to securely support a metal tray for placing the Dutch oven. The flat surface of several cinder blocks also works well in this situation.

Cleaning Up

- Maintain a close eye on your food while cooking so that it doesn't burn. Charred grub is difficult to remove from cookware and requires much more time, water, and detergent during cleanup. Keeping food from burning is perhaps the single most important step for making cleanup easier.

- A pair of large butler basins or storage containers, one filled with sudsy water, the other with rinse water, makes cleanup more efficient.

- A lining of heavy-duty foil in the Dutch oven is excellent for containing messes from gooey recipes. Once the foil is removed following the meal, most of the glop goes with it, making cleanup much easier. Note that foil is not suitable for recipes that require a lot of stirring, because the foil can snag and tear.

- Cleaning greasy cookware and dishes with cold water can be a real challenge to one's patience. Use warm water to cut grease and make cleanup more rapid and hygienic. Place a pot of water over low heat on the stove or campfire to warm for this purpose while the meal is being served. The water will be hot once it's time for cleanup. Carefully pour the hot water into the wash bin, bringing it to a safe temperature with cold water as required.

- Use dishwashing liquid sparingly during cleanup, just enough to do the job. Use only detergents that are biodegradable. As a general rule, don't use detergents on cast iron. (Information specific to cleaning and storing cast iron can be found in the following section.)

- Dirty dishes left to lie will eventually attract bugs and wild animals. To avoid such interest, ensure that all cookware and utensils have been washed and rinsed before leaving camp during the day or when retiring for the evening.

- Dispose of wash and rinse water, also called "gray water," in a manner acceptable for your particular camp. Some camping areas have dedicated gray water disposal stations. Never dump gray water directly into a stream or lake.

Caring for Cast Iron

- For cleanup, cast-iron cookware requires no more than a sponge or dish rag for wiping, a gentle nonmetallic scrub pad or spatula for scraping, warm water for washing, plenty of clean water for rinsing, and a towel for drying. *Metal* scouring pads are a sure way to destroy your cast iron's protective coating and should never be used. Detergents should be avoided unless absolutely necessary, because soap attacks the cast iron's patina (also called its seasoning).

- The warmer the wash water, the more effectively grease can be cut by water alone. When grease is heavy or solidified, and the wash water cold, a *very small* amount of dish soap will make cast-iron cleanup easier. But the outer layer of patina can be compromised in the process. For this reason, use soap sparingly, if ever.

- Never use a dishwasher to clean your cast iron. The strong detergents in a dishwasher can remove so much coating that re-seasoning would be required.

- Some recipes challenge even the best nonstick coating, especially if the food is frozen when first placed in the cookware or accidentally charred while cooking. Soaking cookware in water is the usual remedy for tough stuck-on foods, but cast iron should not be left for long periods in plain water. Otherwise the patina may weaken and rust spots could form. Instead, pour an inch or two of very hot water into the soiled cookware before the residue has a chance to harden. This is a very effective and nondamaging cleaning method. The stubborn food will begin to loosen after just a few minutes. Once the soak water cools to a safe temperature, the residue can be removed with a nonmetallic spatula or scrub pad and the cookware then cleaned and rinsed as usual.

- If a separate cook pot is unavailable to heat wash water, add a shallow pool of clean water to the soiled Dutch oven or skillet and then place it over the campfire, camp stove, or any remaining hot coals. Once the water is hot, *very carefully* move the cast iron to a safe location. As the metal cools to a temperature safe for cleaning, the food residue will have loosened and subsequent cleanup will be much easier.

- When cleaning or drying, *never* allow cast-iron cookware to go completely dry over a fire. The cast iron won't melt or warp, but the patina can quickly turn to ash without the protective influence of the moisture.

- Avoid placing hot cast iron in cool water. The resulting thermal shock may warp or crack the metal. Wait for your cookware to cool to the touch before immersing it in wash water or pouring water into it.

- Use a long-handled wooden or silicone spoon for mixing and stirring in your Dutch oven. Occasional use of metal spoons is acceptable, but avoid sustained use of metal utensils, which can wear the patina over time.

- Rub or spray a thin layer of food-grade oil over the entire surface of your cookware, including the legs and handles, both before using and after each cleaning. Doing so *before* cooking will further build the durability and effectiveness of the nonstick coating. And doing so *after* cleaning will protect the patina and prevent rust during storage. Using paper towels to spread the oil makes the job easier and less messy. *If this important maintenance step is neglected prior to cooking or long-term storage, the protective patina is likely to be damaged and rust will soon form.*

Breakfast

DUTCH OVEN DONUTS

V-LO

Total Servings: 4–6
Preparation Time: 45 minutes
Challenge Level: Moderate

Preparation at Camp:

1. Heat oil in Dutch oven over 25 coals.

2. While oil is warming, use hands to form a hole through the middle of each biscuit, shaping into the form of a donut.

3. Once a drop of water sizzles in the oil, carefully lower donuts into the oven, a few at a time, with a slotted ladle. Cook in small batches.

4. Once donuts are puffed and lightly browned, carefully remove from oil.

5. Transfer donuts to paper towels to drain and cool.

6. Repeat steps 3 through 5 for remaining dough.

7. Pour the sugar into a paper lunch bag.

8. Place cooked donuts in the paper bag containing the sugar and gently shake to coat before serving.

4 cups sunflower oil

1 (12-ounce) container Pillsbury Simply Buttermilk refrigerated biscuits

1 cup granulated sugar

Required Equipment:
10-inch camp Dutch oven

Slotted ladle

Paper lunch bag

> Do not crowd the oven. Otherwise, donuts may stick together.

Jim Landis
New Providence, Pennsylvania

UPSIDE-DOWN PINEAPPLE FRENCH TOAST

V-LO

Total Servings: 4–6
Preparation Time: 1 hour
Challenge Level: Moderate

¼ cup (½ standard stick) butter

⅓ cup brown sugar

1 (8-ounce) can crushed pineapple, drained

4 eggs

1 cup milk

¼ teaspoon salt

6 (1-inch-thick) slices French bread

Required Equipment:
10-inch camp Dutch oven

Medium-size mixing bowl

Preparation at Camp:

1. Melt butter in Dutch oven over 21 coals.

2. Stir brown sugar and pineapple into butter until sugar dissolves.

3. Working quickly, beat eggs, milk, and salt together in bowl.

4. Dip bread slices in egg mixture, allowing bread to soak for about 5 to 10 seconds on each side.

5. Arrange bread slices in Dutch oven over pineapple mixture.

6. Cover oven and transfer 14 coals from under the oven to the lid.

7. Bake for about 30 minutes, until top of French toast is golden brown.

8. Arrange French toast on serving plate and spoon any pineapple mixture remaining in oven over the bread slices.

Jim Landis
New Providence, Pennsylvania

LAZY CAMPER'S CASSEROLE

Total Servings: 6–8
Preparation Time: 1¼ hours
Challenge Level: Easy

Preparation at Camp:
1. In Dutch oven preheated over 21 coals, brown the sausage.

2. Remove Dutch oven from coals, then carefully drain grease. Set oven aside momentarily.

3. Beat eggs in bowl, then add milk, salt, and ground mustard.

4. Stir bread pieces and cheese into egg mixture.

5. Pour egg-bread mixture over sausage in Dutch oven.

6. Cover oven and rearrange coals by moving 14 briquettes to the lid.

7. Bake for about 40 minutes, refreshing coals if required, until eggs congeal. Serve with black pepper to taste.

Donna Pettigrew
Anderson, Indiana

1 pound uncooked Italian sausage

6 eggs

2 cups milk

1 teaspoon salt

½ teaspoon ground mustard

6 slices bread, torn into small pieces

1 cup shredded cheddar cheese

Ground black pepper to taste

Required Equipment:
10-inch camp Dutch oven

Medium-size mixing bowl

SUNRISE HONEY BUNS

V-LO

Total Servings: 6–8
Preparation Time: 2½ hours
Challenge Level: Difficult

Dough:
2 cups unbleached all-purpose flour plus extra for working dough

2 tablespoons dried yeast

1 pinch salt

½ cup honey

¾ cup warm water

½ cup (1 standard stick) butter, softened

1 teaspoon sunflower oil

Filling:
½ cup (1 standard stick) butter, softened

¾ cup honey

1 tablespoon ground cinnamon

Required Equipment:
10-inch camp Dutch oven

2 medium-size mixing bowls

Small rolling pin

Heavy-duty aluminum foil

Preparation at Camp:

1. Combine flour, yeast, salt, ½ cup honey, warm water, and ½ cup butter in bowl.

2. Knead mixture until dough has a uniform consistency. If dough is overly wet and sticky, add flour in small amounts as needed to make it less so.

3. Grease second bowl with oil. Place dough in the second bowl, cover, and place in a warm location for about an hour.

4. While dough is rising, prepare filling by combining ½ cup butter, ¾ cup honey, and cinnamon in now-empty first bowl. Mix well.

5. Once dough is ready, use a floured rolling pin or smooth water bottle to roll dough on a flat surface into a 12 x 10-inch rectangle.

6. Uniformly spread honey-butter filling over dough.

7. Roll dough like a carpet into a 10-inch-long log.

8. Slice log into 8 disks of equal size.

9. Line Dutch oven with greased foil. Arrange all 8 rolls side-by-side on the bottom of the oven, cover oven, then set aside for dough to rise for another 30 minutes.

10. Using 14 coals on the lid and 7 under the oven, bake for 30 to 40 minutes, until tops of rolls are lightly browned.

John Bostick
Cincinnati, Ohio

OSWEGATCHIE FRUITED OATMEAL

Total Servings: 4–6
Preparation Time: 15 minutes
Challenge Level: Easy

V-LO

Preparation at Camp:

1. Bring milk and water to a boil in cook pot.

2. Immediately add oatmeal, brown sugar, dried fruit, and salt.

3. Reduce heat to a simmer and stir for 1 minute.

4. Add cashews, stir, then remove from heat.

5. Top oatmeal with sliced banana and serve.

Option: You can substitute regular oatmeal for the quick oatmeal, but simmer for about 5 minutes longer in step 3.

Ken Harbison
Rochester, New York

2 cups whole milk

1 cup water

1½ cups quick oatmeal

2 teaspoons brown sugar

½ cup dried fruit (your choice)

1 dash salt

⅓ cup cashew pieces

1 banana

Required Equipment:
Small cook pot

BIRD NESTS

Total Servings: 1
Preparation Time: 15 minutes
Challenge Level: Easy

V-LO

1 slice bread

1 tablespoon butter

1 egg

Salt and ground black pepper to taste

Required Equipment:
Small frying pan

Preparation at Camp:

1. Cut a circle from the center of a slice of bread using the rim of a small drinking cup or can as a guide.

2. Melt butter in frying pan over medium heat and place bread in pan.

3. Crack an egg into the hole in the bread.

4. Fry egg and bread together on both sides until egg is cooked through.

5. Serve with salt and black pepper to taste.

Option: *You can substitute a slice of Spam for the bread.*

Don't discard the center cut of bread!
Serve it with jelly.

Ronald G. Behrens
Hawthorn Woods, Illinois

TOASTED ENGLISH MUFFINS

Total Servings: 1
Preparation Time: 15 minutes
Challenge Level: Easy

V-LO

"No toaster? No problem. Toast your English muffins directly in the skillet!"

Preparation at Camp:

1. Warm frying pan over low heat.

2. Spread butter on inside surface of each half of the split muffin.

3. Toast muffin halves, butter side down, in the skillet.

4. Serve once butter side becomes lightly browned.

1 English muffin, split

1 tablespoon butter, softened

Required Equipment:
Small frying pan

Christine and Tim Conners
Statesboro, Georgia

PRINCESS VIOLET'S NUTELLA DELIGHT

Total Servings: 1
Preparation Time: 15 minutes
Challenge Level: Easy

V-LO

"Car camping with three young girls calls for quick cooking and fun. I came up with this recipe on our last trip. It kept the girls busy while I made the coffee!"

1 tablespoon cream cheese, softened

1 tablespoon Nutella Hazelnut Spread, softened

2 slices bread

½ banana, sliced into thin disks

1 teaspoon butter, softened

Preparation at Camp:

1. Spread cream cheese and Nutella on one slice of bread.

2. Push banana slices into the cream cheese-Nutella.

3. Cover cream cheese-Nutella-banana with the second slice of bread.

4. Butter the outside face of each slice of bread.

5. In a skillet over medium heat, fry sandwich on both sides until golden brown.

Required Equipment:
Small frying pan

This recipe can also be cooked in a pie iron or in foil over a grill or campfire.

Princess Violet
Sultan, Washington

EGG MUFFINS

Total Servings: 1
Preparation Time: 15 minutes
Challenge Level: Easy

V-LO

Preparation at Camp:

1. Slice bacon into 2 shorter pieces, then cook in frying pan until crisp.

2. Fry the egg.

3. Split English muffin. To the bottom half, add cooked bacon, followed by cheese slice, then the cooked egg.

4. Cover egg with top of muffin, then loosely wrap the sandwich in foil.

5. Place foil packet on a grate over a grill, campfire, or stove to toast, cooking both sides for a few minutes before serving.

1 slice bacon

1 egg

1 English muffin

1 slice cheese (your choice)

Required Equipment:
Small frying pan

Heavy-duty aluminum foil

Katie Salyer Cox
Tucson, Arizona

VAGABOND VEGGIE OMELET

Total Servings: 2
Preparation Time: 30 minutes
Challenge Level: Moderate

V-LO

1/4 cup (4 tablespoons) olive oil

1 Roma tomato, chopped

1 bell pepper, chopped

3 green onions, chopped

1/4 cup chopped fresh dill

4 eggs

2 teaspoons milk

Salt and ground black pepper to taste

1/4 cup shredded cheese (your choice)

Required Equipment:
Medium-size frying pan

Small bowl

Medium-size mixing bowl

Spatula

Preparation at Camp:

1. Warm 2 tablespoons olive oil in frying pan over medium heat.

2. Add tomato, bell pepper, green onion, and dill to the pan, then sauté for about 5 minutes, until bell pepper softens.

3. Transfer cooked vegetables to a small bowl and set aside.

4. Whisk eggs and milk in medium-size bowl for about 1 minute. Season with salt and black pepper to taste.

5. Carefully wipe the frying pan, then add 1 tablespoon olive oil to the pan and return to medium heat for a few moments to warm the oil.

6. Pour half of the egg mixture into the frying pan, rotating and tilting pan so that the liquid covers the entire bottom of the pan to an even depth. Return pan to the stove.

7. Once eggs are cooked partly through, evenly spread about half of the vegetable mixture over one side of the eggs, then top the vegetables with half of the shredded cheese.

8. Continue to cook until cheese melts and egg fully sets.

9. Using the spatula, flip the half of the omelet not covered by vegetables over that part of the omelet that is.

10. Transfer omelet to serving plate, then repeat steps 5 through 9 for the second omelet.

Christine and Tim Conners
Statesboro, Georgia

BRECKENRIDGE BREAKFAST BURRITOS

Total Servings: 4
Preparation Time: 30 minutes
Challenge Level: Easy

Preparation at Camp:

1. Melt butter in frying pan over medium heat.

2. Add sausage and potatoes to pan, stir, and cook until potatoes are heated through.

3. Crack eggs into the frying pan and scramble.

4. Once eggs are fully cooked, remove pan from heat and divide contents among 4 tortillas.

5. Cover egg mixture on each tortilla with cheese and optional salsa, then roll each like a burrito and serve.

Option: *You can substitute 10 ounces of precooked breakfast sausage, chopped into small pieces, for the Tyson sausage crumbles.*

Jim Landis
New Providence, Pennsylvania

¼ cup (½ standard stick) butter

1 (10-ounce) package Tyson fully cooked breakfast sausage crumbles

2 cups frozen regular shredded hash browns, thawed

4 eggs

4 large flour tortillas

½ cup shredded cheese (your choice)

Optional: salsa to taste

Required Equipment:
Medium-size frying pan

CALIFORNIA DREAMER SCRAMBLED EGGS

V-LO

Total Servings: 4–6
Preparation Time: 15 minutes
Challenge Level: Easy

8 eggs

½ cup milk

1 (10.75-ounce) can condensed cream of mushroom soup

2 tablespoons butter

Salt and ground black pepper to taste

Preparation at Camp:

1. Whisk eggs with milk in a bowl.

2. Add soup to bowl and whisk briefly.

3. Melt butter in a frying pan over medium heat.

4. Add egg mixture to pan and scramble until eggs become firm.

5. Serve with salt and black pepper to taste.

Required Equipment:
Medium-size frying pan

Medium-size mixing bowl

*Donna Pettigrew
Anderson, Indiana*

Photo by Scott Simerly

CORNED BEEF SCRAMBLE

Total Servings: 4–6
Preparation Time: 15 minutes
Challenge Level: Easy

Preparation at Camp:
1. Warm oil in a frying pan over medium heat.
2. Sauté onion and bell pepper until onion becomes translucent.
3. Add beef hash to the pan, then crack eggs over hash. Sprinkle shredded cheese over all.
4. Scramble until eggs are fully cooked.
5. Serve with salt and black pepper to taste.

Christine and Tim Conners
Statesboro, Georgia

2 tablespoons olive oil

1 onion, chopped

1 bell pepper, chopped

1 (15-ounce) can corned beef hash

4 eggs

1 cup shredded sharp cheddar cheese

Salt and ground black pepper to taste

Required Equipment:
Medium-size frying pan

BAUERN FRÜHSTÜCK (FARMER'S BREAKFAST)

Total Servings: 4–6
Preparation Time: 30 minutes
Challenge Level: Easy

"A warm and hearty southern German breakfast to kick-start a great day outdoors."

2 tablespoons sunflower oil

1 pound boneless cooked ham, cubed

1 (14.5-ounce) can diced new potatoes, drained

1 bell pepper, chopped

1 onion, chopped

6 eggs

2 Roma tomatoes, chopped

Salt, ground black pepper, and garlic powder to taste

Required Equipment:
Medium-size frying pan

Medium-size mixing bowl

Preparation at Camp:

1. Heat oil in a skillet over medium heat.

2. Add ham, potatoes, bell pepper, and onion to the skillet. Sauté until onions become translucent.

3. Whisk eggs in a bowl, then pour into skillet.

4. Add tomatoes to the pan.

5. Stir continuously, as if scrambling, until eggs are fully set.

6. Serve with salt, black pepper, and garlic powder to taste.

Michael Kaiserauer
Berlin, Germany

WHOLE WHEAT BLUEBERRY PANCAKES

Total Servings: 4–6
Preparation Time: 30 minutes
Challenge Level: Easy

V-LO

Preparation at Camp:

1. Combine flour, salt, sugar, and baking powder in a mixing bowl. Stir well.

2. Whisk eggs in a cup and add to flour mixture in bowl along with the milk.

3. Stir batter to remove all large clumps.

4. Melt butter in a frying pan over medium heat.

5. Pour batter into pan, using about ½ cup for each pancake. Do not overcrowd the pan, giving batter adequate room to spread.

6. Set about 10 blueberries in the batter for each pancake.

7. Once bubbles begin forming in the batter, flip the cake immediately, cooking only briefly on the opposite side before removing from the pan.

8. Repeat steps 5 through 7 for remaining batter.

9. Serve pancakes with maple syrup to taste.

1½ cups whole wheat flour

1 teaspoon salt

2 tablespoons granulated sugar

2 teaspoons baking powder

2 eggs

2 cups milk

2 tablespoons butter

1 cup fresh blueberries

Maple syrup to taste

Required Equipment:
Medium-size mixing bowl

Medium-size frying pan

Christine and Tim Conners
Statesboro, Georgia

MOUNTAIN DEW PANCAKES

Total Servings: 4–6
Preparation Time: 30 minutes
Challenge Level: Easy

V-LO

"Pancakes so delicious, you'll want to save them for dessert!"

2 eggs

1/4 cup (1/2 standard stick) butter, softened

2 cups Mountain Dew soda

1/2 teaspoon vanilla extract

2 tablespoons sour cream

1 teaspoon salt

1 1/2 teaspoons baking powder

1/3 cup granulated sugar

2 cups all-purpose flour

Pancake syrup or whipped cream to taste

Required Equipment:
Medium-size mixing bowl

Medium-size frying pan

Preparation at Camp:
1. Whisk eggs in a bowl.

2. Stir in softened butter, Mountain Dew, vanilla extract, sour cream, salt, baking powder, sugar, and flour. Do not overwork the batter. Some lumps are OK.

3. Grease frying pan and warm over medium heat.

4. Using about 1/4 cup for each pancake, pour batter into pan, allowing room for batter to spread. Do not overcrowd skillet with too many pancakes at a time.

5. Once bubbles appear on the surface of the cakes, immediately flip, then briefly cook on the opposite side before transferring to a serving plate.

6. Repeat steps 4 and 5 with remaining batter.

7. Serve pancakes with syrup or whipped cream to taste.

Option: *The batter also works great for deep-frying fish.*

John Malachowski
Stewartstown, Pennsylvania

BOB'S SURPRISE

Total Servings: 6–8
Preparation Time: 30 minutes
Challenge Level: Easy

"I was taught this recipe by my former Scoutmaster, Bob Rayle."

Preparation at Camp:

1. Whisk eggs in a bowl and set aside.

2. Brown sausage in a frying pan over medium heat until cooked through. Drain grease, then return pan to the flame.

3. Add potatoes, onion, and bell pepper to the pan and cook until onions become translucent.

4. Pour eggs into the pan along with the mushrooms and scramble until eggs are fully set and excess liquid has evaporated. Remove pan from heat.

5. Lay cheese slices over the top of the eggs and cover until cheese melts.

6. Serve with salt and black pepper to taste.

Greg Moore
Trussville, Alabama

8 eggs

1 pound uncooked Italian sausage

1 (14.5-ounce) can diced new potatoes, drained

1 large onion, diced

1 large green bell pepper, chopped

1 (4-ounce) can mushroom pieces and stems, drained

½ pound extra-sharp cheddar cheese, sliced

Salt and ground black pepper to taste

Required Equipment:
Medium-size mixing bowl

Large frying pan with cover

LEMON CREPES

V-LO

Total Servings: 4–6
Preparation Time: 45 minutes
Challenge Level: Difficult

"An unusual sight on any campout, crepes are like very thin pancakes and can be made savory with herbs or sweet with sugar and vanilla. This recipe goes with the latter. Hey, even Mountain Man Mike has a softer side."

1 cup milk

4 eggs

¼ teaspoon kosher salt

1 tablespoon granulated sugar

½ teaspoon pure vanilla extract

1 cup all-purpose flour

1 small lemon

½ cup (1 standard stick) butter, softened

1 (10-ounce) jar lemon curd

¼ cup confectioners' sugar

Required Equipment:
Medium-size mixing bowl

Small metal mixing bowl or cup

Small frying pan

Preparation at Camp:

1. Combine milk, eggs, salt, sugar, and vanilla extract in a medium-size bowl. Whisk into a smooth liquid.

2. Slowly add flour to the bowl and continue to whisk until the batter is very thin with no clumps.

3. Squeeze juice from lemon into a small metal bowl or cup. Combine with ½ stick of softened butter. Warm bowl or cup over gentle heat to melt butter.

4. Preheat a small frying pan over medium-high heat.

5. Add a small amount of the melted lemon-butter mixture, enough to barely coat the bottom of the pan.

6. Pour in about ¼ cup crepe batter, enough to just cover the pan as the batter is swirled around.

7. Once the top of crepe is dry, immediately twirl and shake pan to loosen the crepe.

8. Using wrist action, flip the crepe over. If crepe has trouble loosening, gently flip it using a spatula.

9. Cook for just a few moments on the other side before transferring crepe to a plate.

10. Spread about 1½ tablespoons lemon curd in a thin layer on the crepe, then roll crepe into a log.

11. Brush a small amount of the melted lemon-butter onto the crepe and shake a little confectioners' sugar over it.

12. Repeat steps 5 through 11 for remaining batter.

Mike "Mountain Man Mike" Lancaster
Clovis, California

Photo by Scott Simerly

PRALINE FRENCH TOAST

V-LO

Total Servings: 6–8
Preparation Time: 30 minutes
Challenge Level: Moderate

1 (1-pound) loaf French bread

8 eggs

3/4 cup milk

1 teaspoon vanilla extract

1/4 cup (1/2 standard stick) butter

1 cup chopped pecans

1 cup maple syrup

Required Equipment:
Medium-size mixing bowl

Large frying pan

Small frying pan

Preparation at Camp:

1. Cut bread into 3/4-inch-thick slices.

2. Combine eggs, milk, and vanilla extract in a bowl and whisk well.

3. In a large frying pan, melt some of the butter over medium heat.

4. Working in small batches, dip slices of bread into egg mixture, one at a time, coating both sides.

5. Fry bread on both sides until golden brown.

6. Repeat steps 3 through 5 until all bread slices are cooked.

7. In a small frying pan, roast pecans in a small amount of butter over medium heat for a few minutes.

8. Pour maple syrup over pecans, stir well to coat, then remove pecans from heat.

9. Serve French toast with maple-pecan-butter syrup.

Christine and Tim Conners
Statesboro, Georgia

OUTER BANKS SHRIMP 'N GRITS

Total Servings: 6–8
Preparation Time: 30 minutes
Challenge Level: Moderate

"We make several camping trips each year with friends, taking turns cooking meals and trying out new recipes. This one was invented during an October visit to the Outer Banks of North Carolina, perfect for the coastal waters and cool breeze. It is easy to prepare, and the flavors are out of this world."

Preparation at Camp:

1. Bring cream and broth to a boil in cook pot, then immediately reduce heat to low.

2. Add grits to the pot, stir, and continue to cook until grits thicken, about 5 minutes.

3. Stir cheese and butter into grits until melted, then remove pot from heat.

4. Fry bacon in a frying pan, then add green onion, garlic, bell pepper, and shrimp.

5. Sauté shrimp mixture for 2 to 3 minutes, until shrimp turns pink.

6. Serve by pouring shrimp sauté over grits.

Scott Simerly
Apex, North Carolina

1 cup heavy cream

1 (14.5-ounce) can beef broth

1 cup quick grits

1/3 cup shredded pepper Jack cheese

1 tablespoon butter

3 slices thick bacon, chopped

2 green onions, chopped

1 clove garlic, minced

1/2 red bell pepper, diced

12 ounces shrimp, peeled

Required Equipment:
Medium-size cook pot

Medium-size frying pan

ENCAMPMENT BREAKFAST

V-LO

Total Servings: 1
Preparation Time: 15 minutes
Challenge Level: Easy

2 slices regular-size
bread

2 teaspoons butter

1 egg

Salt and ground black
pepper to taste

Optional: slice of cheese
(your choice)

Required Equipment:
Pie iron

Preparation at Camp:

1. Butter one side of each slice of bread.

2. Place a slice of bread in one side of the pie
    iron, butter-side against the cast iron.

3. Crack egg over center of bread.

4. Sprinkle egg with salt and black pepper to
    taste, then cover with optional cheese.

5. Cover with second slice of bread, butter-
    side up.

6. Close pie iron and cook over campfire coals,
    about 5 minutes per side, until bread is
    lightly toasted and the egg cooked through.

Donna Pettigrew
Anderson, Indiana

PAPER BAG BACON AND EGGS

Total Servings: 1
Preparation Time: 15 minutes
Challenge Level: Easy

Preparation at Camp:

1. Cut bacon strips in half across the length and lay pieces side-by-side in the bottom of a paper lunch bag. If the bag is not sturdy, double up using a bag within a bag.

2. Crack two eggs into the bag over the bacon.

3. Roll the top of the bag in flattened sections as you would the end of a tube of toothpaste and skewer it closed with a camping fork so that the bag hangs at the end of the fork.

4. Toast the food in the bag by holding it with the fork above hot coals, being careful not to set the bag on fire. The rendered bacon fat will be absorbed by the paper and protect the bag from burning. The bag shouldn't drip unless it's torn.

5. Once the eggs become firm, set bag aside to cool for a few minutes, then carefully tear the bag open to make a bowl. Serve breakfast straight from the bag!

2 thick strips bacon

2 eggs

Required Equipment:
Paper lunch bags

Camping fork

If the paper trash will be burned in the campfire following breakfast, reduce the risk of wildfire by first tearing the used lunch bag into small pieces or by weighing the bag down once it is in the fire. This will decrease the tendency of the burning ash to float away.

Georgia Bosse
Portland, Oregon

EGGS IN AN ORANGE

V-LO

Total Servings: 1
Preparation Time: 15 minutes
Challenge Level: Easy

1 large orange

2 eggs

Salt and black pepper to taste

Required Equipment:
Heavy-duty aluminum foil

Preparation at Camp:

1. Slice orange in half then scoop out and eat the contents.

2. Remove any remaining citrus bits, leaving the rind intact.

3. Place each rind "bowl" on a separate large square of foil.

4. Crack an egg into each of the bowls.

5. Sprinkle eggs with salt and black pepper to taste.

6. Wrap foil around each orange rind, being careful not to tilt the bowls.

7. Placed wrapped oranges directly onto the hot embers of a campfire.

8. Cook oranges for 3 to 5 minutes, depending on the desired firmness.

Jim Landis
New Providence, Pennsylvania

APPLE MOUNTAIN TURNOVERS

V-LO

Total Servings: 1
Preparation Time: 15 minutes
Challenge Level: Easy

Preparation at Camp:

1. Spread cream cheese on one side of a slice of bread and lay in a greased pie iron, cream cheese side facing up.

2. Add apple slices to cream cheese, then sprinkle apples with cinnamon and sugar.

3. Cover with the second bread slice.

4. Close pie iron and hold over campfire for about 5 to 10 minutes, rotating occasionally, until apples are soft and hot.

Kelly Weir
Mobile, Alabama

2 slices bread

1 tablespoon cream cheese

1/4 apple, cored, peeled, and sliced into thin wedges

1/2 teaspoon ground cinnamon

1/2 teaspoon confectioners' sugar

Required Equipment:
Pie iron

EGG-ON-A-STICK

V-LO

Total Servings: 1
Preparation Time: 15 minutes
Challenge Level: Moderate

"My husband and I have used this recipe many times. It really works!"

1 egg

Salt and ground black pepper to taste

Required Equipment:
Green stick, 2 to 3 feet long, no more than ¼ inch in diameter at end

Preparation at Camp:

1. With the sharp tip of a knife, bore a small hole through the shell in an end of the egg.

2. Insert end of stick through the hole and into the egg, being careful not to crack the shell. Do not drive the stick all the way through the egg.

3. Carefully bore a second, very small hole through the shell on the end opposite the first hole. Do not skip this step! This second hole serves as a steam vent to prevent the egg from exploding while it cooks.

4. Suspend the stick above the campfire flame or embers for about 6 minutes. The shell should char and cooked egg white may protrude from the holes.

5. Carefully remove eggshell and serve with salt and black pepper to taste.

Some shrubs and trees are toxic! Exercise caution when selecting a cooking stick for this recipe.

Reduce impact by using only branches collected from the ground and, then, only in areas where downed wood is plentiful and gathering is permitted.

Tina Welch
Harper, Kansas

PHOENIX'S EGG

V-LO

Total Servings: 1
Preparation Time: 15 minutes
Challenge Level: Moderate

"Which came first, the Phoenix or the egg?"

Preparation at Camp:

1. With the sharp tip of a knife, bore a small hole through the shell in one end of the egg. Do not skip this step! The hole serves as a steam vent to prevent the egg from exploding while it cooks.

2. Using tongs, carefully set egg directly into the hot embers of the fire, with the end of the egg containing the vent hole facing upward.

3. Allow egg to cook for no more than 5 minutes before removing from the fire.

4. Carefully peel egg, then serve with salt and black pepper to taste.

1 egg

Salt and ground black pepper to taste

Required Equipment:
Long-handled tongs

> The egg is likely to char if cooked in open flames or within a furnace-like recess deep in the campfire. Such zones will be much hotter than a more open area of embers free of steady flames.

Donna Pettigrew
Anderson, Indiana

WORMY APPLE

Total Servings: 1
Preparation Time: 45 minutes
Challenge Level: Easy

1 medium-size apple

1 precooked sausage link

Maple syrup to taste

Required Equipment:
Heavy-duty aluminum foil

Preparation at Camp:

1. Core apple, removing a central cylinder without cutting the apple in half.

2. Insert sausage link into the open core of the apple.

3. Wrap apple-sausage tightly in foil.

4. Place wrapped apple on a bed of hot coals for about 30 minutes.

5. Remove apple from coals and carefully unwrap.

6. Drizzle apple-sausage with maple syrup to taste and serve.

Avoid using a roaring fire for cooking the wrapped apple. Otherwise, the intense heat will char the apple. Instead, the coal bed of a spent campfire is ideal for this, or any, foil cooking.

Jim Landis
New Providence, Pennsylvania

CINNAMON BREAKFAST PIE

V-LO

Total Servings: 2
Preparation Time: 30 minutes
Challenge Level: Moderate

Preparation at Camp:

1. Unroll crescent dough before it warms and becomes sticky.

2. Spread dough from 2 crescent rolls into each side of greased pie iron, using dough from 4 crescents total.

3. Mold dough to fill and fit both sides of pie iron.

4. Spread half of the butter over dough.

5. Sprinkle half of the cinnamon and half of the brown sugar over the butter.

6. Close pie iron and cook over campfire, turning frequently, for about 5 minutes or until dough becomes golden brown.

7. Allow iron to cool for a few minutes, then repeat steps 2 through 6 for the second pie using the remaining ingredients.

1 (8-ounce) container original Pillsbury Crescent Rolls

2 tablespoons butter, softened

2 teaspoons ground cinnamon

2 teaspoons brown sugar

Required Equipment:
Pie iron

> This recipe cooks quickly and burns easily, so pay close attention to cooking time.

Tom Cartwright
Euclid, Ohio

POP TORTES

V-LO

Total Servings: 2
Preparation Time: 15 minutes
Challenge Level: Moderate

"This is what happens when a camper has a toaster pastry but no toaster! I was on a canoe expedition. It was cold, and I really wanted to toast my blueberry pastry when I noticed that my buddy had brought along some foil. A few ingredients later, I was making my first 'pop tortes.'"

2 tablespoons jam (your choice) or honey

2 unfrosted fruit toaster pastries

2 tablespoons Nutella Hazelnut Spread

1 dash cinnamon

Required Equipment:
Heavy-duty aluminum foil

2 sturdy sticks, at least 12 inches long

Preparation at Camp:

1. Spread jam or honey on one side of the first pastry.

2. On one side of the second pastry, spread the Nutella.

3. Sprinkle cinnamon over the jam or honey.

4. Make a "sandwich" by placing one pastry on top of the other, with the jam or honey and Nutella spreads on the inside of the "sandwich" facing each other.

5. Set pastry sandwich on a large square of foil.

6. Lay a stick next to each of the long sides of the pastry sandwich, two total.

7. Tightly wrap the pastry sandwich in foil, adjusting the stick positions so that they both protrude from one side of the foil package. The sticks will serve as handles, and the tightly wrapped foil will hold the sticks firmly in place.

8. Using the sticks, hold foil package over campfire until pastries are heated through, toasting for a few minutes on each side.

9. Carefully unwrap, divide in half, and serve.

Options: Try almond butter, peanut butter, or soy nut butter instead of Nutella.

To prepare as a dessert, add a few mini marshmallows to the Nutella before closing the "sandwich."

The pastries can also be toasted over a camp stove
using chopsticks as handles.

Curt "The Titanium Chef" White
Forks, Washington

Photo by Scott Simerly

Lunch

CAMP DUTCH OVEN RICE PIZZA

Total Servings: 4–6
Preparation Time: 45 minutes
Challenge Level: Easy

"Easy to make and easy to clean up!"

Preparation at Camp:

1. In Dutch oven over 21 coals, brown ground beef until no pink remains. Drain any excess fat.

2. Stir pizza sauce and water into the oven and bring to a boil.

3. Add rice to the oven along with any optional topping ingredients, then stir.

4. Remove oven from heat once rice is tender, about 10 minutes.

5. Top the rice with cheese. Cover oven and set aside to rest a few minutes for cheese to melt before serving.

Option: *You can substitute Italian sausage for the ground beef.*

Duane Ripperger
Amarillo, Texas

1 pound lean ground beef

1 (15-ounce) jar pizza sauce

$3/4$ cup water

1 cup instant rice

Optional: pizza toppings such as mushrooms, bell peppers, onions, olives, fresh basil, pineapple, Italian seasoning, fennel seeds, pepperoni

1 cup shredded mozzarella cheese

Required Equipment:
10-inch camp Dutch oven

GRANDMA'S SOUP

Total Servings: 8
Preparation Time: 45 minutes
Challenge Level: Easy

1 pound lean ground beef

1 (15-ounce) can Veg-All, drained

1 (15-ounce) creamed corn

1 (15-ounce) can green beans, drained

1 (15-ounce) can black beans, drained and rinsed

1 (46-ounce) bottle original V8 juice

¼ cup (½ standard stick) butter

Salt and ground black pepper to taste

Preparation at Camp:

1. Brown ground beef in Dutch oven over 21 briquettes.

2. Carefully drain grease, then return oven to the coals.

3. Add remaining ingredients to oven and bring soup to a low boil.

4. Season with salt and black pepper to taste, then serve.

Option: Simmer the soup for an extended period of time to further enhance the flavor.

*Jessica Keeley
Statesboro, Georgia*

Required Equipment:
10-inch camp Dutch oven

QUICK CLAM CHOWDER

Total Servings: 4–6
Preparation Time: 15 minutes
Challenge Level: Easy

Preparation at Camp:

1. Combine all ingredients in a pot.

2. Warm chowder over medium heat for 10 to 15 minutes, then serve.

Christine and Tim Conners
Statesboro, Georgia

2 (10-ounce) cans whole baby clams, undrained

4 green onions, chopped

1 (15-ounce) can diced new potatoes, drained

1 (15-ounce) can corn, drained

2 tablespoons butter

1 (12-ounce) can evaporated milk

1/4 teaspoon salt

Ground black pepper to taste

Required Equipment:
Medium-size cook pot

TAHQUAMENON FALLS PENNE PEPPERONCINI

V-LO

Total Servings: 6–8
Preparation Time: 30 minutes
Challenge Level: Moderate

"Named for one of my favorite parks in Michigan."

1 (16-ounce) package penne rigate pasta

1 (8-ounce) jar pesto sauce

1 (12-ounce) jar pepperoncini peppers, drained, stemmed, and sliced

1 (7-ounce) jar sliced pitted green olives, drained and sliced

2 (2.25-ounce) cans sliced black olives, drained

3 ounces sun-dried tomatoes, chopped

¼ cup chopped fresh basil

1 (6-ounce) jar grated Romano cheese

Required Equipment:
Large cook pot

Medium-size frying pan

Large mixing bowl

Preparation at Camp:

1. Cook pasta in pot according to package directions. Drain pasta and set aside.

2. Combine pesto sauce, peppers, olives, and tomatoes in a frying pan.

3. Simmer pesto mixture over low heat, stirring occasionally, until heated through.

4. In a large bowl, combine cooked pasta with pesto mixture. Toss.

5. Top pasta with fresh basil and Romano cheese, then serve.

Julie Kibler
Statesboro, Georgia

DR PEPPER BEANS

Total Servings: 6–8
Preparation Time: 45 minutes
Challenge Level: Easy

Preparation at Camp:
1. Combine all ingredients in a pot.

2. Bring ingredients to a boil, then immediately reduce heat to a simmer.

3. Continue to cook for about 30 minutes before serving.

Scott Simerly
Apex, North Carolina

1 (28-ounce) can pork and beans

1 small onion, chopped

1 tomato, chopped

1 bell pepper, chopped

1/2 cup brown sugar

1/2 teaspoon ground cloves

1 (8-ounce) can crushed pineapple, drained

1/2 pound summer sausage, chopped

1/2 (12-ounce) can Dr Pepper soda

Required Equipment:
Medium-size cook pot

LENTIL SOUP

Total Servings: 8
Preparation Time: 45 minutes
Challenge Level: Easy

1 (16-ounce) package dried lentils, rinsed

8 cups water

2 unpeeled red potatoes, cubed

1 pound hot dogs, thinly sliced

1 white onion, diced

2 tablespoons white vinegar

4 regular-size chicken bouillon cubes

Salt and ground black pepper to taste

Required Equipment:
Medium-size cook pot

Preparation at Camp:

1. Bring lentils and water to a boil, then add remaining ingredients.

2. Reduce heat to a simmer and stir.

3. Cover pot and continue to cook for about 30 minutes, until lentils and potatoes are soft.

Michael Kaiserauer
Berlin, Germany

BARBECUE BLEU SANDWICH

Total Servings: 1
Preparation Time: 15 minutes
Challenge Level: Easy

Preparation at Camp:

1. Lay meat and cheese on one of the bread slices.

2. Spread barbecue sauce on one side of the second slice of bread.

3. Cover the cheese and meat with the second slice of bread, barbecue sauce facing the meat and cheese.

4. Butter the outside face of each slice of bread.

5. Fry sandwich in covered frying pan over low heat, lightly toasting each side before serving with optional mustard.

Ken Harbison
Rochester, New York

2 ounces Oscar Mayer Carving Board Ham

2 ounces Oscar Mayer Carving Board Chicken Breast

1 slice Swiss cheese

2 slices bread

1 tablespoon barbecue sauce

$1/2$ tablespoon butter, softened

Optional: prepared mustard to taste

Required Equipment:
Small frying pan with lid

CARIBBEAN QUESADILLA

Total Servings: 3–5
Preparation Time: 30 minutes
Challenge Level: Moderate

1 small onion, chopped

1 small jalapeño, chopped

4 tablespoons sunflower oil

1 (8-ounce) can crushed pineapple, drained

1 (10-ounce) can water-packed chunk chicken, drained

3 tablespoons barbecue sauce

6 medium-size whole wheat tortillas

1 cup shredded Colby-Jack cheese

Optional: fresh cilantro to taste, finely chopped

Required Equipment:
Medium-size frying pan

Small mixing bowl

Spatula

Preparation at Camp:

1. In a frying pan over medium heat, cook onion and jalapeño in 1 tablespoon oil until onion is translucent.

2. Add pineapple, chicken, and barbecue sauce to the pan. Stir thoroughly, warm for a few minutes, then transfer chicken mixture to a bowl.

3. Carefully wipe skillet, then warm 1 tablespoon oil over medium-low heat.

4. Add a tortilla to the pan, then cover it with about one-third of the chicken mixture along with 1/3 cup shredded cheese. Add optional cilantro at this time.

5. Cover chicken-cheese with a second tortilla.

6. Fry until bottom tortilla is lightly toasted, carefully flipping and doing the same to the other tortilla.

7. Repeat steps 3 through 6 to make 2 more quesadillas.

8. Slice quesadillas into wedges, then serve.

Shelby Mullinax
Statesboro, Georgia

TREKKER'S TACOS

Total Servings: 4
Preparation Time: 15 minutes
Challenge Level: Easy

Preparation at Camp:

1. Brown ground beef in a frying pan over medium heat until no pink remains. Drain grease.

2. Return pan to stove, add water to beef, and stir in the taco seasoning mix.

3. With chip bags still sealed, carefully crush corn chips in the bag.

4. Slice each chip bag open along a side.

5. Divide beef mix, lettuce, tomato, cheese, salsa, and sour cream among the 4 bags.

6. Enjoy tacos straight from the bag.

Millie Hutchison
Pittsburgh, Pennsylvania

1 pound lean ground beef

³/₄ cup water

1 (1.25-ounce) package taco seasoning mix

4 (2-ounce) single-serving packages corn chips

1 cup shredded lettuce

1 tomato, chopped

1 cup shredded cheddar cheese

¹/₄ cup salsa

¹/₄ cup sour cream

Required Equipment:
Medium-size frying pan

ADIRONDACK BURRITOS

Total Servings: 6
Preparation Time: 30 minutes
Challenge Level: Easy

1 tablespoon olive oil

1 pound lean ground beef

1 (15-ounce) can kidney beans, drained

1½ cups quick-cooking rice

1 (16-ounce) jar salsa

1 (14-ounce) can chicken broth

6 large whole wheat tortillas

Optional: lettuce, tomatoes, onions, shredded cheese, hot sauce, sour cream

Required Equipment:
Large frying pan

Preparation at Camp:

1. Warm oil in a frying pan over medium heat, then brown the beef until no pink remains. Drain any excess grease.

2. Add beans, rice, salsa, and chicken broth to the pan. Stir.

3. Bring mixture to a boil, then reduce heat to a simmer.

4. Continue to cook, stirring occasionally, until rice is tender, about 10 minutes.

5. Remove pan from heat and divide the beef mixture among the 6 tortillas.

6. Cover the beef mixture with optional toppings, then wrap like a burrito and serve.

Rick Pickelhaupt
Amherst, New York

BAVARIAN BRATS

Total Servings: 1
Preparation Time: 15 minutes
Challenge Level: Easy

Preparation at Camp:

1. Slice brat lengthwise about three-quarters of the way through.

2. Stuff brat with sauerkraut.

3. Wrap brat in bacon, like a stripe on a candy cane, beginning on one end and finishing on the other. Fasten bacon to brat with toothpicks.

4. Cook brat on a camping fork over campfire. Brat will be ready to serve once bacon turns crispy.

5. Eat brat from the fork or with optional bun and mustard.

1 stadium-style precooked brat

1 tablespoon sauerkraut

1 thin slice bacon

Optional: bun, stone-ground mustard

Required Equipment:
Camping fork

Toothpicks

Option: You can substitute a hot dog for the brat, stuffing it with cheese and serving it with ketchup.

*Donna Pettigrew
Anderson, Indiana*

PIE IRON PIZZA

Total Servings: 1
Preparation Time: 15 minutes
Challenge Level: Easy

1 tablespoon butter

2 slices bread

1 tablespoon pizza sauce

4 slices pepperoni

1 slice mozzarella cheese

Required Equipment:
Pie iron

Preparation at Camp:
1. Spread butter on one side of each slice of bread.

2. Set bread slices in the pie iron with the buttered sides against the iron surface.

3. Spread pizza sauce on one slice of bread then add pepperoni and cheese.

4. Close the pie iron and cook over the campfire for about 10 minutes, turning occasionally, until bread is toasted.

> If bread slices are too large for the pie iron, trim to fit before buttering.

Ken and Judy Harbison
Rochester, New York

NORTHWEST RIVER CURRY

Total Servings: 2
Preparation Time: 30 minutes
Challenge Level: Easy

"It's that time of year: cool, crisp mornings and freshness in the air. All that's needed to make it perfect: a roaring fire and a savory meal to bring in the warmth of home."

Preparation at Camp:

1. Tear off a large square of aluminum foil and pull up the 4 corners to make a bowl.

2. Add rice and curry powder to the foil bowl, then pour in soup. Gently stir to mix, being careful not to tear foil.

3. Lay chicken strips and asparagus pieces over the rice.

4. Pull foil corners together and seal the pouch tightly. Be sure to keep the opening of the pouch facing upward to keep liquid from leaking.

5. Place pouches on a grate close to the embers over a campfire or on a grill set at medium heat.

6. Cook for about 10 to 15 minutes, until no trace of pink remains in the meat.

1/2 cup instant white rice

1 teaspoon yellow curry powder

1 (10.75-ounce) can condensed cream of mushroom soup

1 uncooked boneless chicken breast, cut into 1/4-inch-thick strips

5 stalks asparagus, chopped into 1-inch-long pieces

Required Equipment:
Heavy-duty aluminum foil

Option: *You can substitute cream of celery or cream of broccoli for the mushroom soup.*

Kimberly Yost
Virginia Beach, Virginia

FUNKY CAMPFIRE PIZZA

Total Servings: 3–4
Preparation Time: 15 minutes
Challenge Level: Moderate

²/₃ cup barbecue sauce

1 (14-ounce) precooked pizza crust

1 small onion, chopped

1 (6-ounce) package Tyson Grilled & Ready Chicken Breast Strips

1 cup shredded cheddar-Jack cheese

Required Equipment:
Heavy-duty aluminum foil

Preparation at Camp:

1. Spread barbecue sauce over pizza crust.

2. Top pizza with onion, chicken, and cheese, spreading uniformly over the top.

3. Place pizza directly on a clean grate over embers in the campfire or grill. Do not set pizza too close to the embers or in open flames!

4. Tent a large sheet of foil into a dome over the pizza. The foil dome will act as a reflector oven.

5. Cook pizza 7 to 10 minutes, depending on proximity to the heat, until cheese is melted. Check often to avoid burning the pizza crust.

6. Slice and serve.

Matt Lamas
Bel Air, Maryland

MOUNTAIN MAN MIKE'S SHRIMP POUCHES

Total Servings: 4
Preparation Time: 30 minutes
Challenge Level: Easy

"Everybody loves a meal that is not only great tasting but also fun to make. When it comes to cooking, what could be more fun than wrapping your lunch in foil then tossing it over an open fire? Foil cooking uses a technique called 'steaming,' where a little liquid in the foil pouch poaches the food."

Preparation at Camp:

1. Divide each of the noodle "bricks" from a pack of ramen in half. Place each on a large square of foil, 4 total.

2. Evenly divide mushrooms, shrimp, green onions, crushed red pepper, and salt among the 4 pouches, stacking the ingredients on the noodle bricks.

3. In a small bowl combine water, rice wine, soy sauce, and sesame oil. Stir well.

4. Pull up the corners of each of the 4 pouches to form bowls, then drizzle soy-oil liquid evenly over the noodles in each.

5. Fold the corners of each foil square together, tightly sealing each of the pouches.

6. Place packets on a grate over the campfire or grill. Be sure to keep each pouch opening facing upward so that the liquid doesn't drain from pouch.

7. Cook for about 10 minutes, until noodles are soft and shrimp is pink.

Option: *If no cooking grate is available, place foil packs directly onto coals or embers, but reduce the cooking time and pay closer attention to prevent burning.*

2 (3-ounce) packages ramen noodles, flavor packs removed

1/2 pound fresh mushrooms, chopped

1 (12-ounce) package large raw shrimp, peeled

12 green onions, chopped

1/2 teaspoon crushed red pepper

1/2 teaspoon salt

1/2 cup water

1/2 cup Japanese rice wine (mirin)

2 tablespoons soy sauce

1/4 cup sesame oil

Required Equipment:
Heavy-duty aluminum foil

Small mixing bowl

Mike "Mountain Man Mike" Lancaster
Clovis, California

HIGH NOON HAM AND SWISS LOAF

Total Servings: 6–8
Preparation Time: 15 minutes
Challenge Level: Easy

1 (1-pound) loaf French bread

3 (4.25-ounce) cans deviled ham spread

1 green onion, chopped

⅓ cup mayonnaise

4 ounces shredded Swiss cheese

1 (2-ounce) jar pimientos, drained

Required Equipment:
Small mixing bowl

Heavy-duty aluminum foil

Preparation at Camp:

1. Slice bread diagonally, part way through the loaf, into ½-inch-thick slices, but do not cut bread all the way through. All slices should remain intact for now.

2. In a bowl combine deviled ham, onion, mayonnaise, cheese, and pimientos. Stir well.

3. Evenly divide ham filling among every other slice in the loaf. These will be cut apart in a later step to form individual sandwiches.

4. Wrap loaf securely in foil.

5. Set foil packet on grate over campfire or grill, about 4 inches from the heat.

6. Warm for about 10 minutes, until cheese is melted.

7. Unwrap packet, cut individual sandwiches from the loaf, and serve.

Millie Hutchison
Pittsburgh, Pennsylvania

FLYING PIGS

Total Servings: 8
Preparation Time: 15 minutes
Challenge Level: Easy

Preparation at Camp:

1. Press pairs of triangular crescent roll dough together to make 4 rectangular dough shapes.

2. Cut each rectangle in half to make 8 squares.

3. Set a hot dog on top of each square. Sprinkle with optional cheese.

4. Roll dough around hot dog, pinching the dough closed.

5. Skewer hot dog on a camping fork and heat over embers until dough becomes golden brown, about 10 minutes.

6. Serve with optional ketchup.

1 (8-ounce) container original Pillsbury Crescent Rolls

8 hot dogs

Optional: shredded cheese, ketchup

Required Equipment:
Camping forks

Donna Pettigrew
Anderson, Indiana

MRS. RUBLE'S SPECIAL SLOPPY JOES

Total Servings: 8
Preparation Time: 1 hour
Challenge Level: Easy

Patty Mix:
1½ pounds lean ground beef

1½ cups bread crumbs

¾ cup sweetened condensed milk

1 large onion, diced

1 teaspoon salt

1 dash ground black pepper

1 egg, beaten

Sauce Mix:
2¼ cups ketchup

1½ tablespoons Worcestershire sauce

⅓ cup brown sugar

3 tablespoons white vinegar

8 hamburger buns

Required Equipment:
Medium-size bowl

Large frying pan

Small bowl

Aluminum pan

Aluminum foil

Preparation at Camp:

1. Knead patty ingredients together in a medium-size bowl.

2. Form ground beef mixture into 8 patties.

3. In a large frying pan over high heat, quickly brown patties on both sides. Do not fully cook the meat at this point. It will finish cooking over the campfire.

4. In a small bowl, blend sauce ingredients together.

5. Transfer patties to an aluminum pan and pour sauce over the patties.

6. Cover aluminum pan with foil and place on grate over campfire or grill.

7. Simmer meat for about 45 minutes, checking to be sure the meat is fully cooked before removing from heat.

8. Serve on hamburger buns.

Ed Bedford
Chapel Hill, North Carolina

MEXICAN PIZZA

Total Servings: 2
Preparation Time: 15 minutes
Challenge Level: Easy

V-LO

Preparation at Camp:

1. Tear off two large squares of foil, each slightly larger than a tortilla.

2. Rub top side of both foil pieces with sunflower oil.

3. Place a tortilla on each of the 2 greased sheets of foil.

4. Divide pizza sauce between the 2 tortillas, spreading evenly on each.

5. Add optional pizza toppings to each tortilla, then divide shredded cheese between both.

6. With each tortilla uncovered on top of its foil sheet, place on grill over medium heat, then cook until cheese has melted, about 10 minutes.

1 teaspoon sunflower oil

2 large flour tortillas

1 (5-ounce) packet Boboli pizza sauce

Optional: pizza toppings such as olives, mushrooms, onions, pepperoni

1/2 cup shredded Mexican-style cheese

Required Equipment:

Heavy-duty aluminum foil

You can also cook Mexican pizza on a grate over a campfire, but you will have to pay closer attention to be sure the tortilla doesn't scorch. Alternately, you can fold the tortillas in half, place on an oiled frying pan, then heat until cheese melts, flipping once.

Melissa Seacat
Salem, Indiana

WORM BURGERS

Total Servings: 4
Preparation Time: 30 minutes
Challenge Level: Easy

"This recipe puts a fun spin on plain old hamburgers and is sure to make everyone at camp giggle and squirm. The juice from the meat swells the noodles while grilling, causing them to hang out of the burgers like juicy worms!"

1 pound ground beef

½ cup dried chow mein noodles

Salt and ground black pepper to taste

4 hamburger buns

Toppings: cheese, tomatoes, lettuce, onions, ketchup, mayonnaise, mustard

Required Equipment:
Medium-size mixing bowl

Preparation at Camp:

1. Combine beef and chow mein noodles in a bowl. Add salt and black pepper to taste.

2. Gently knead ingredients to combine, then form mixture into 4 patties.

3. Grill burgers to taste and serve on buns with toppings of choice.

Donna Pettigrew
Anderson, Indiana

SANTA FE CHICKEN SANDWICH

Total Servings: 4
Preparation Time: 30 minutes
Challenge Level: Easy

"Just like what you might find at a Southwestern-style fast-food restaurant, but with less fat."

Preparation at Camp:

1. Cut each chicken breast horizontally, nearly all the way through the meat, then fold open so that each will be able to cover a bun once cooked.

2. Place chicken breasts in a quart-size ziplock bag with teriyaki glaze. Knead chicken breasts to coat.

3. In a small bowl, combine dressing ingredients and stir well.

4. Grill chicken breasts over medium heat until cooked through, about 5 to 8 minutes per side. Juice should run clear when cut, with no trace of pink, and internal meat temperature should be at least 165°F.

5. Meanwhile, toast buns on the grill, if desired.

6. Spread about 1 tablespoon dressing inside each bun. To each bun, add 2 leaves lettuce and about a quarter of the chilies.

7. Place cooked chicken breast on the chilies, then top with a slice of cheese. Cap with the top of the bun and serve.

Ken Harbison
Rochester, New York

4 small skinless boneless chicken breasts

4 tablespoons glaze-style teriyaki sauce

4 large whole-grain hamburger buns or Kaiser rolls

8 lettuce leaves

1 (4-ounce) can chopped mild green chilies

4 slices cheddar or Jack cheese

Dressing:
4 tablespoons light mayonnaise

$1/2$ teaspoon chili powder

$1/4$ teaspoon curry powder

1 dash ground cayenne pepper

Required Equipment:
Quart-size ziplock bag

Small mixing bowl

GRILLED PIZZA

Total Servings: 6
Preparation Time: 30 minutes
Challenge Level: Easy

6 English muffins

1 (5-ounce) packet Boboli pizza sauce

4 ounces pepperoni slices

6 slices mozzarella cheese

Required Equipment:
Heavy-duty aluminum foil

Preparation at Camp:

1. Slice each English muffin in half.

2. Evenly divide pizza sauce among 6 muffin halves, spreading the sauce evenly over the coarse side of each half.

3. Divide pepperoni slices equally among the 6 muffin halves, arranging the slices over the pizza sauce.

4. Lay a slice of mozzarella over the pepperoni on each of the muffin halves.

5. Cover each pizza with its other muffin half, then securely wrap each in foil.

6. Place wrapped pizzas on a grill over medium heat, cooking for about 10 minutes per side, until cheese has melted.

> You can also cook wrapped muffin pizzas on a grate over the campfire.

Christine and Tim Conners
Statesboro, Georgia

ENGLISH BARBECUE

Total Servings: 6
Preparation Time: 30 minutes
Challenge Level: Easy

Preparation at Camp:

1. Slice each English muffin in half.

2. Divide barbecue sauce evenly among 6 muffin halves, about 2 teaspoons each, spreading the sauce evenly over the coarse side of each half.

3. Divide chicken equally among the 6 muffin halves, arranging meat over the barbecue sauce.

4. Lay a slice of provolone over the chicken on each of the muffin halves.

5. Cover each muffin base with its other half, then securely wrap each in foil.

6. Place wrapped sandwiches on a grill over medium heat, cooking for about 10 minutes per side, until cheese has melted.

6 English muffins

¼ cup barbecue sauce

1 (10-ounce) can water-packed chunk chicken, drained

6 slices provolone cheese

Required Equipment:
Heavy-duty aluminum foil

> You can also cook wrapped sandwiches on a grate over the campfire.

Christine and Tim Conners
Statesboro, Georgia

HIKER'S SALAD

Total Servings: 1
Preparation Time: 15 minutes
Challenge Level: Easy

1 golden delicious or red apple

1 tablespoon peanut butter

1 tablespoon raisins

Required Equipment:
Small mixing bowl

Preparation at Camp:

1. Carefully core the apple from the top, leaving the bottom intact.

2. Mix peanut butter and raisins in a small bowl, then transfer to the cavity in the apple.

3. Eat "salad" as you would a regular apple.

> You can prepare this easy apple salad in camp, then wrap it in foil for a snack while hiking.

Delano LaGow
Oswego, Illinois

POUCH PITA POCKETS

Total Servings: 2
Preparation Time: 15 minutes
Challenge Level: Easy

"Meat and fish are now available in convenient foil pouches, virtually devoid of the extraneous fluids found in the canned versions. Foil pouch meats taste better, too."

Preparation at Camp:

1. Mix fish, relish, mayonnaise or salad dressing, and celery in a small bowl.

2. Cut each pita in half, then open a pocket in each.

3. Cut each slice of cheese in half and insert a piece into each of the 4 pockets.

4. Equally divide the fish mixture among the 4 pockets and serve.

Option: *You can substitute pouch turkey or chicken for the fish.*

Ken and Judy Harbison
Rochester, New York

1 (3-ounce) foil pouch water-packed tuna or salmon

2 tablespoons pickle relish

2 tablespoons light mayonnaise or salad dressing

1 small stalk celery, diced

2 pitas

2 slices provolone cheese

Required Equipment:
Small mixing bowl

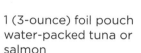

BLACK BEAR BEAN SALAD

Total Servings: 4–6
Preparation Time: 15 minutes
Challenge Level: Easy

2 (15-ounce) cans black
beans, drained and
rinsed

1 (15-ounce) can sweet
corn, drained

6 green onions,
chopped

1 jalapeño pepper, diced

2 tablespoons honey

Juice of 2 limes

¼ cup olive oil

¼ teaspoon salt

1 bunch cilantro,
trimmed and finely
chopped

2 Roma tomatoes,
chopped

1 ripe avocado, chopped

Ground black pepper to
taste

Required Equipment:
Medium-size mixing
bowl

Preparation at Camp:

1. Combine all ingredients in a bowl.

2. Toss and serve.

Christine and Tim Conners
Statesboro, Georgia

BUNGEE JUMPER'S BEAN SALAD

V

Total Servings: 4–6
Preparation Time: 45 minutes
Challenge Level: Easy

Preparation at Camp:

1. Combine all ingredients in a bowl.

2. Stir well and cover.

3. Place bowl on ice in a cooler. Allow to rest for about 30 minutes to marinate and chill before serving.

Christine and Tim Conners
Statesboro, Georgia

1 (14.5-ounce) can cut green beans, drained

1 (15-ounce) can kidney beans, rinsed and drained

1 (14.5-ounce) can wax beans, drained

3 stalks celery, chopped

1 small sweet onion, chopped

1/2 teaspoon garlic salt

1/2 cup granulated sugar

1/4 cup white vinegar

1/4 cup sunflower oil

1/2 teaspoon salt

1 (2-ounce) jar pimientos, drained

Required Equipment:
Medium-size mixing bowl

MOJO MANGO SALSA

Total Servings: 4–6
Preparation Time: 1 hour
Challenge Level: Easy

"Awesome with blue corn tortilla chips!"

2 ripe mangoes, peeled and cut into small pieces

1 (15.25-ounce) can unsweetened sliced pineapple, drained and chopped

2 jalapeño peppers, chopped

1 bunch cilantro, trimmed and chopped

1 small red onion, diced

Juice of 1 key lime

1 tablespoon granulated sugar

½ teaspoon salt

Ground black pepper to taste

1 (18-ounce) package tortilla chips

Required Equipment:
Medium-size mixing bowl

Preparation at Camp:

1. In a bowl, combine all ingredients, except for the tortilla chips. Toss well.

2. Cover and set bowl in a cooler to chill for about 45 minutes.

3. Serve with tortilla chips.

Christine and Tim Conners
Statesboro, Georgia

PBJ ROLLS-UPS

Total Servings: 6
Preparation Time: Less than 5 minutes
Challenge Level: Easy

"Here is an easy, pack-friendly way to bring sandwiches along on your day hikes while camping."

Preparation at Camp:

1. Divide peanut butter and jelly evenly among tortillas.

2. Spread the peanut butter and jelly, then fold and roll the tortillas.

Cap Cresap
Saugus, California

2 (9-ounce) containers Skippy Squeeze It Peanut Butter

1 (16-ounce) squeeze container jelly (your choice)

1 (12-count) package medium-size flour tortillas

Required Equipment:
None

DAHLONEGA DEVILED HAM SANDWICHES

Total Servings: 6
Preparation Time: 15 minutes
Challenge Level: Easy

2 (4.25-ounce) cans
deviled ham spread

¼ cup mayonnaise

1 (8-ounce) package
cream cheese, softened

1 small onion, diced

1 (2-ounce) jar
pimientos, drained

12 slices bread

Required Equipment:
Small mixing bowl

Preparation at Camp:
1. Combine deviled ham, mayonnaise, cream cheese, onion, and pimientos in a bowl. Stir to blend.

2. Divide ham mixture among 6 slices of bread, top each with another slice of bread, then serve.

Option: *Toast sandwiches in a frying pan with a little butter before serving.*

Christine and Tim Conners
Statesboro, Georgia

EASY CAMP FRUIT SALAD

Total Servings: 6–8
Preparation Time: 45 minutes
Challenge Level: Easy

Preparation at Camp:

1. Cut fruit into bite-size pieces, then transfer to a large bowl.

2. Pour crushed pineapple and its juice over fruit.

3. Sprinkle Jell-O powder over fruit, then toss to mix well.

4. Cover and allow fruit to rest for about 20 minutes before serving.

Options: Any fruit should work for this recipe. Here are some of the more popular selections: apples, pears, grapes, strawberries, other berries, bananas, cantaloupe, honeydew melon, mandarin oranges, kiwis, mangoes, watermelon, cherries, papayas, peaches, and nectarines.

4 pounds cored, peeled, and pitted fresh fruit (your choice)

1 (20-ounce) can crushed pineapple

1 (3-ounce) package raspberry or strawberry-flavored Jell-O

Required Equipment:
Large mixing bowl

Rikki Webb
Hampton, Virginia

Dinner

WILD BOAR WITH VEGGIES

Total Servings: 2
Preparation Time: 1¼ hours
Challenge Level: Easy

"One of our favorite campout meals."

Preparation at Camp:

1. Melt butter in a Dutch oven set over 19 coals.

2. Brown pork chops on both sides. Chops do not require thorough cooking during this step. Momentarily remove chops from oven.

3. Add carrots, green beans, and cubed potatoes to the oven. Lay chops on top of the vegetables.

4. Combine soup mix with water in a cup, stir well, then pour over the chops.

5. Sprinkle chops with basil.

6. Cover the Dutch oven. Redistribute coals, transferring 13 to the lid.

7. Bake for about 45 minutes, until carrots and potatoes are soft. Refresh coals as required.

Brian Penrod
Ossian, Indiana

1 tablespoon butter

2 pork chops

1 carrot, peeled and chopped into ½-inch pieces

½ cup trimmed 1-inch green bean pieces

1 medium red potato, chopped into small cubes

1 (1-ounce) packet Lipton Recipe Secrets Onion Recipe Soup and Dip Mix

⅔ cup water

½ teaspoon dried basil

Required Equipment:
10-inch camp Dutch oven

DUTCH OVEN CORNISH GAME HENS

Total Servings: 4–6
Preparation Time: 1¼ hours
Challenge Level: Easy

2 (about 1.5-pound) Cornish game hens

1 onion, sliced

3 carrots, peeled and cut into 1-inch pieces

2 red potatoes, cubed

1 (14.5-ounce) can chicken broth

Salt and ground black pepper to taste

Required Equipment:
10-inch camp Dutch oven

Preparation at Camp:

1. Set hens in a Dutch oven.

2. Arrange vegetables around hens.

3. Pour chicken broth over all.

4. Put lid on the oven. Using 16 coals on the lid and 7 under the oven, bake for about 1 hour, until skin is golden and internal temperature of meat is at least 165°F. Refresh coals as required.

5. Serve with salt and black pepper to taste.

Mike Donnell
Memphis, Tennessee

CHICKEN CHUTNEY

Total Servings: 4–6
Preparation Time: 1¼ hours
Challenge Level: Easy

Preparation at Camp:
1. Set chicken in Dutch oven and pour chutney over the top. Place lid on the oven.

2. Using 21 coals on the lid and 10 under the oven, bake chicken for about 1 hour, until the meat is fully cooked with an internal temperature of at least 165°F. Refresh coals as required.

1 whole chicken

1 (9-ounce) jar Major Grey's Chutney

Required Equipment:
12-inch camp Dutch oven

The deeper interior of larger Dutch ovens, such as the 12-inch specified here, is usually required to cook whole birds or larger cuts of meat. However, chopping the chicken into smaller pieces prior to cooking, or using a smaller bird, will permit use of a smaller Dutch oven. Whatever your method, do not force a cut of meat to fit within an oven! If you do, any pieces of meat in contact with the underside of the lid will burn.

Christine and Tim Conners
Statesboro, Georgia

CAJUN GOOP

Total Servings: 4–6
Preparation Time: 1¼ hours
Challenge Level: Easy

"I got hooked on jambalaya during a trip to New Orleans. Once home, I began experimenting with different recipes until I had one I really enjoyed. I then adapted it to the Dutch oven. Scouts from the troop I'm involved with love the recipe despite the title they've given it!"

2 tablespoons sunflower oil

1 boneless chicken breast, cut into bite-size pieces

1 pound smoked sausage, cut into bite-size pieces

1 large onion, chopped

3 stalks celery, chopped

1 bell pepper, chopped

2 cloves garlic, minced

1 (14.5-ounce) can chicken or beef stock

1 heaping teaspoon salt

1 dash ground cayenne pepper

2 tablespoons paprika

1 cup long-grain rice

1 bunch green onions, chopped

Required Equipment:
10-inch camp Dutch oven

Preparation at Camp:

1. Warm oil in a Dutch oven over 21 coals.

2. Brown the chicken, then add the sausage, sautéing both meats for an additional 5 minutes.

3. Add onion, celery, bell pepper, and garlic to the oven and cook until vegetables are tender.

4. Pour stock into oven, then add salt and cayenne pepper. Bring to a gentle boil. Refresh coals if required, but don't allow boil to become vigorous.

5. Add paprika and rice to the oven, stir, then cover. Simmer for 15 to 20 minutes.

6. Add green onions to the oven, replace lid, and continue cooking for an additional 10 minutes, or until rice becomes tender.

Lawrence Bernstein
Mount Prospect, Illinois

APPLESAUCE PORK LOINS

Total Servings: 4–6
Preparation Time: 1¼ hours (plus 2 hours for marinating)
Challenge Level: Easy

"This is a camp-friendly version of a recipe from my friend, Chris Hegele. He will often cook fifty to sixty pounds of applesauce pork loins at a time for church dinners!"

Preparation at Camp:

1. Mix dry rub ingredients together in a medium-size bowl.

2. Place pork in bowl with dry rub, covering meat with seasoning and gently pressing so that seasoning clings to the pork.

3. Cover bowl and chill in cooler for about 2 hours.

4. Transfer chilled loin to a Dutch oven, cover, and cook for 30 minutes using 16 coals on the lid and 7 under the oven.

5. Mix topping ingredients together in a small bowl.

6. Flip loin in oven, then cover pork with the topping.

7. Continue to cook pork for an additional 30 minutes, refreshing coals as required, until meat is cooked through and has a minimum internal temperature of 145°F.

8. Slice loin, spooning applesauce topping over the meat, then serve.

Option: *The leftover pork loin sauce is excellent on garlic mashed potatoes.*

Scott Simerly
Apex, North Carolina

1½ pounds pork loin

Dry Rub:
3 tablespoons brown sugar

1 tablespoon salt

1 tablespoon Italian seasoning

1 tablespoon ground black pepper

1 tablespoon garlic powder

2 teaspoons ground rosemary

Topping:
3 cups applesauce

3 tablespoons brown sugar

1 tablespoon ground cinnamon

2 teaspoons ground nutmeg

1 teaspoon ground cloves

Required Equipment:
Medium-size mixing bowl

10-inch camp Dutch oven

Small mixing bowl

RAGING RIVER SPARERIBS

Total Servings: 4–6
Preparation Time: 2¼ hours
Challenge Level: Easy

2 pounds boneless
spareribs

½ cup ketchup

1 teaspoon salt

2 tablespoons white
vinegar

1 small onion, chopped

1 tablespoon
Worcestershire sauce

½ cup water

2 tablespoons brown
sugar

1 teaspoon ground
mustard

Required Equipment:
10-inch camp Dutch
oven

Small mixing bowl

Preparation at Camp:

1. Cut ribs into serving-size pieces and set in a Dutch oven.

2. Combine remaining ingredients in a small bowl, stir well, then pour over ribs. Place lid on oven.

3. Using 16 coals on the lid and 7 under the oven, cook ribs for about 2 hours. Refresh coals as needed.

Jim Landis
New Providence, Pennsylvania

PRISON FOOD

Total Servings: 6–8
Preparation Time: 1 hour
Challenge Level: Easy

"This recipe came about as I was trying to find a way to make cornbread and chili without dirtying a second Dutch oven. The name 'Prison Food' was given to it by my son's Boy Scout patrol when they prepared it on a camping trip without completely reading through the instructions. They mixed all the ingredients together, and, after baking it, thought it looked like 'prison food,' whatever that is."

Preparation at Camp:

1. In a Dutch oven over 21 coals, brown ground beef with onion. Drain excess grease.

2. Stir salsa and beans into the ground beef and onions.

3. While salsa and beans warm, combine muffin mix, egg, and milk in a bowl. Stir well.

4. Pour corn muffin batter over beef and vegetables in the oven, then sprinkle cheese over the batter.

5. Place cover on oven and transfer 14 coals from under the oven to the lid.

6. Bake for 25 to 30 minutes, refreshing coals if required.

Bob Valinski
Flemington, New Jersey

1 pound lean ground beef

1 onion, chopped

1 (16-ounce) jar salsa

1 (15-ounce) can kidney beans, drained and rinsed

1 (8.5-ounce) package Jiffy corn muffin mix

1 egg

⅓ cup milk

1 cup shredded Mexican-style cheese

Required Equipment:
10-inch camp Dutch oven

Small mixing bowl

SUMMIT SHEPHERD'S PIE

Total Servings: 6–8
Preparation Time: 1¼ hours
Challenge Level: Easy

3 cups instant Hungry Jack Mashed Potatoes

4 cups milk

1 teaspoon salt

1 pound lean ground beef

1 teaspoon Old Bay seasoning

1 onion, diced

Optional: ground black pepper to taste

1 (15-ounce) can corn, drained

1 (15-ounce) can peas, drained

Required Equipment:
Medium-size mixing bowl

10-inch camp Dutch oven

Preparation at Camp:

1. In a bowl, mix instant mashed potatoes with milk and salt, then stir well. Set aside for the moment.

2. Combine ground beef, Old Bay, onion, and optional black pepper to taste in a Dutch oven over 21 coals.

3. Brown the ground beef, then drain any excess grease.

4. Add corn and peas to the Dutch oven and stir, covering all with mashed potatoes.

5. Rearrange coals, transferring 14 to the lid.

6. Bake for about 40 minutes, until top of potatoes acquire a light-brown crust. Refresh coals as required.

Derrick Tryon
Ephrata, Pennsylvania

BAKED TACO STACK

Total Servings: 6–8
Preparation Time: 1¹/₂ hours
Challenge Level: Easy

Preparation at Camp:

1. In a Dutch oven over 21 coals, brown ground beef along with taco seasoning mix.

2. Remove oven from coals, drain excess grease, and remove meat to a bowl, setting it aside for the moment.

3. Place a tortilla on the bottom of the oven and cover it with about one-quarter of the cooked beef, salsa, chilies, cottage cheese, and Mexican-style cheese blend.

4. Add another tortilla and repeat by covering with another quarter of the toppings.

5. Repeat step 4 twice more, then finish with the final tortilla on top. Place the lid on the oven.

6. Redistribute the coals, transferring 14 briquettes to the lid. Bake for about 40 minutes, refreshing coals as required.

Larry Michaels
Arnold, Missouri

1 pound lean ground beef

1 (1-ounce) packet taco seasoning mix

5 (10-inch) flour tortillas

1 (16-ounce) jar salsa

1 (4-ounce) can diced green chilies

1 (24-ounce) container cottage cheese

1 pound shredded Mexican-style cheese blend

Required Equipment:
10-inch camp Dutch oven

Medium-size mixing bowl

CHUCKWAGON STEW

Total Servings: 6–8
Preparation Time: 3$\frac{1}{4}$ hours
Challenge Level: Moderate

"This is a hearty one-pot meal that takes hunger and body slams it!"

1 pound boneless chuck, brisket, rump, round, or flank beef, trimmed and cubed

1 tablespoon olive oil

1 clove garlic, chopped

1$\frac{3}{4}$ cups water, divided

1 (14.5-ounce) can whole stewed tomatoes

1 thin slice lemon

1 medium onion, cut into wedges

$\frac{1}{2}$ tablespoon salt

1 dash ground black pepper

1$\frac{1}{2}$ tablespoons granulated sugar

4 medium carrots, peeled and cut into chunks

3 potatoes, peeled and cut into chunks

1 dash ground cloves

$\frac{1}{4}$ teaspoon dried basil

1 (15-ounce) can peas, drained

3 tablespoons all-purpose flour

Required Equipment:
10-inch camp Dutch oven

Small mixing bowl

Preparation at Camp:

1. In a Dutch oven over 21 coals, brown cubed beef in oil. Meat is not to be cooked through in this step.

2. Drain all but about 3 tablespoons grease from the oven.

3. Add garlic, 1$\frac{1}{2}$ cups water, tomatoes, lemon slice, onion, salt, black pepper, and sugar to the oven.

4. Mix ingredients well, then cover oven and redistribute briquettes, transferring 14 coals to the lid.

5. Refreshing coals as needed, cook for about 2 hours, then add carrots, potatoes, cloves, and basil.

6. Continue to cook for about 45 minutes, then add peas.

7. In a small bowl, combine flour with remaining $\frac{1}{4}$ cup water, mix well, then stir into stew.

8. Heat for a few more minutes, then serve.

Mike "Mountain Man Mike" Lancaster
Clovis, California

CALICO COWBOY BEANS

Total Servings: 8
Preparation Time: 1¹/₂ hours
Challenge Level: Easy

"While backpacking with friends in Glacier National Park years ago, one of the hikers in the group shared this 'secret recipe' with me. I've used it on camping trips with my high school students ever since. I've found that cooking with a Dutch oven over a coal fire is a new experience for most of them."

Preparation at Camp:

1. Preheat a Dutch oven over 21 coals, then fry bacon and onion until onion is translucent.

2. Add ground beef or venison to the oven and brown the meat. Carefully drain about three-quarters of the grease.

3. Add remaining ingredients, stir well, and cover oven with lid.

4. Continue to cook for about 45 minutes, stirring occasionally and using only enough coals to produce a gentle simmer. Refresh coals as needed.

William Fjetland
Algona, Iowa

¹/₄ pound bacon, chopped

1 large onion, chopped

1 pound lean ground beef or venison

¹/₂ cup ketchup

¹/₂ cup packed brown sugar

1 tablespoon prepared yellow mustard

4 teaspoons white vinegar

1 (15-ounce) can butter beans, drained and rinsed

1 (15-ounce) can kidney beans, drained and rinsed

1 (15-ounce) can northern beans, drained and rinsed

1 (28-ounce) can pork and beans

Required Equipment:
10-inch camp Dutch oven

DUTCH OVEN MEAT LOAF

Total Servings: 8–10
Preparation Time: 1³/₄ hours
Challenge Level: Easy

2 pounds lean ground beef

1 pound ground pork

2 cloves garlic, minced

1 large onion, diced

1 teaspoon salt

1 teaspoon ground black pepper

¹/₂ teaspoon ground thyme

¹/₂ cup plain bread crumbs

2 eggs

1 pound bacon

2 (8-ounce) cans tomato sauce

Required Equipment:
10-inch camp Dutch oven

Large mixing bowl

Heavy-duty aluminum foil

Preparation at Camp:

1. Line a Dutch oven with foil.

2. Mix all ingredients, except for bacon and tomato sauce, in a large bowl.

3. Knead beef mixture well and form into a loaf.

4. Lay half the bacon strips on top of the foil, covering an area the size of the loaf.

5. Set loaf on the bacon strips and arrange remaining bacon over the top of the loaf. Place lid on the oven. Be sure the loaf and bacon do not make contact with the inside surface of the lid.

6. Using 18 coals on the lid and 9 under the oven, bake for 1 hour, refreshing coals as needed.

7. Remove lid and pour tomato sauce over the loaf.

8. Replace lid and continue to cook for about 15 more minutes. Ensure that the internal temperature of the loaf is at least 160°F before serving.

Option: Goes great with instant garlic mashed potatoes.

Ursula Valentine
Massapequa, New York

LUAU SAUSAGE AND RICE

Total Servings: 4–6
Preparation Time: 15 minutes
Challenge Level: Easy

Preparation at Camp:

1. Combine all ingredients, except rice, in a pot, then stir.

2. Heat mixture to boiling, then add rice and contents of seasoning packet from the rice mix package.

3. Reduce heat to a simmer, stir well, then cover pot.

4. Rice will be tender and the dish ready to serve in 5 to 10 minutes.

> Be sure to use the "Fast Cook Recipe" version of the Uncle Ben's rice mix. The regular version takes much longer to cook.

Jim Landis
New Providence, Pennsylvania

1 pound kielbasa sausage, sliced in half lengthwise then cut into 1-inch pieces

1 green bell pepper, chopped

1 red bell pepper, chopped

1 (8-ounce) can pineapple chunks, undrained

1/2 cup pineapple preserves

2 tablespoons butter

1 1/4 cups water

1 (6.2-ounce) package Uncle Ben's Long-Grain and Wild Rice Fast Cook Recipe rice mix

Required Equipment:
Medium-size cook pot

ROTINI WITH FRESH HERBS

Total Servings: 4–6
Preparation Time: 30 minutes
Challenge Level: Easy

V-LO

"This dish is great anytime, but especially on warm summer evenings."

1 pound rotini pasta

¼ cup extra-virgin olive oil

¼ cup pine nuts

1 tablespoon chopped fresh parsley

1 tablespoon chopped fresh basil

1 tablespoon chopped capers

1 pint cherry tomatoes, chopped

1 cup grated Parmesan cheese

Salt and ground black pepper to taste

Required Equipment:
Large cook pot

Large mixing bowl

Preparation at Camp:

1. Bring water to boil in a cook pot. Add pasta and cook according to package directions; drain.

2. Combine remaining ingredients in a large bowl, then stir.

3. Add cooked pasta to seasoned oil mixture in the bowl, toss well, and serve.

Beverly Jo Antonini
Morgantown, West Virginia

MOM'S SPAGHETTI CARBONARA

Total Servings: 4-6
Preparation Time: 30 minutes
Challenge Level: Moderate

Preparation at Camp:

1. Heat 2 tablespoons oil over medium heat in a frying pan. Add garlic and crushed red pepper, then salt and black pepper to taste.

2. Sauté garlic until softened, but not brown, then transfer from pan to a small bowl.

3. Add remaining oil to the pan and return heat to medium. Sauté the prosciutto until lightly browned. Transfer prosciutto to the bowl with the garlic.

4. Meanwhile, cook pasta in a cook pot according to package directions until al dente. Drain noodles, reserving 1 cup starchy liquid.

5. Set heat to low. With noodles still in the pot, add prosciutto-garlic mixture.

6. Add 1 cup Parmesan cheese to the pot, along with half of the reserved starchy water.

7. Add beaten eggs to the pot and very quickly toss to coat the pasta before the eggs set. Add remaining starchy water in small amounts to keep pasta moist while egg cooks.

8. Toss occasionally for a few more minutes, then top the pasta with parsley and the remaining Parmesan cheese.

4 tablespoons olive oil, divided

6 cloves garlic, minced

1/4 teaspoon crushed red pepper

Salt and ground black pepper to taste

10 ounces prosciutto, chopped

1 pound thin spaghetti noodles

1 1/2 cups grated Parmesan cheese, divided

2 eggs, beaten

1 tablespoon dried parsley

Required Equipment:
Medium-size frying pan

Small mixing bowl

Large cook pot

James Dodd Jr.
Saint James, New York

HAWAIIAN RICE

Total Servings: 4–6
Preparation Time: 45 minutes
Challenge Level: Moderate

"This recipe was inspired by my travels to the Hawaiian Islands, where rice, fresh fruit, and Spam are all very popular."

1 (14-ounce) can coconut milk

2¼ cups water

1 dash ground cardamom

1 dash ground cloves

1 dash ground cinnamon

1 dash turmeric

½ teaspoon salt

2 cups jasmine rice

1 (7-ounce) can Spam, cut into small cubes

1 teaspoon sunflower oil

1 (8-ounce) can crushed pineapple, undrained

1 mango, peeled and diced into small cubes

Required Equipment:
Medium-size cook pot

Small frying pan

Preparation at Camp:

1. In a cook pot, combine coconut milk and water, then add seasonings.

2. Bring liquid to a boil, stirring often.

3. Add rice to the pot, stir, then cover, reducing heat to a simmer.

4. Cook rice for about 20 minutes, until liquid is absorbed.

5. While rice cooks, brown Spam in oil over medium heat in a frying pan.

6. Add fried Spam, pineapple, and mango to the rice in the pot and stir.

7. Remove pot from heat and allow to rest for about 10 minutes before serving.

Curt "The Titanium Chef" White
Forks, Washington

BUBBLE AND SQUEAK

Total Servings: 4–6
Preparation Time: 1 hour
Challenge Level: Easy

"Bubble and Squeak is an English pub food made with cabbage and potatoes, usually spicy meat, and sometimes other vegetables or a cream sauce. There are as many varieties of B&S in England as there are of chili in the United States."

Preparation at Camp:

1. Slice cabbage into 2-inch-thick wedges, then slice again into smaller, 1/2-inch-thick wedges. Discard core and crumble the remaining cabbage into individual pieces, so no longer clinging together.

2. Cut sausage through lengthwise, then chop into smaller pieces.

3. Sauté diced onion in oil in bottom of the cook pot.

4. Add cabbage, sausage, cubed potatoes, black pepper, salt to taste, and 1/2 cup water to pot. Stir and tightly cover.

5. Cook over low heat until potatoes are soft, about 30 to 40 minutes.

1 small head cabbage

1 pound smoked sausage

1 large onion, diced

1 tablespoon olive oil

1 pound red potatoes, cut into small cubes

1 teaspoon ground black pepper

Salt to taste

1/2 cup water

Required Equipment:
Medium-size cook pot with lid

Ken Stanish
Glen Ellyn, Illinois

MACKINAC ISLAND SPAGHETTI

Total Servings: 6–8
Preparation Time: 30 minutes
Challenge Level: Moderate

1 pound spaghetti noodles

1 pound lean ground beef

1 medium onion, chopped

3 cloves garlic, minced

1 bell pepper, chopped

1 (24-ounce) jar spaghetti sauce

1 tablespoon Italian seasoning

Optional: 1 cup shredded mozzarella cheese, grated Parmesan cheese to taste

Required Equipment:
Large cook pot

Large frying pan

Preparation at Camp:

1. Cook noodles in a cook pot according to package directions until al dente. Drain noodles and set aside.

2. Meanwhile, in a frying pan over medium heat, brown ground beef, onion, and garlic until meat is no longer pink.

3. Add bell pepper and spaghetti sauce to the pan, then simmer until pepper becomes tender.

4. Mix Italian seasoning and optional mozzarella into the sauce. Stir and simmer for a few more minutes.

5. Serve sauce over noodles and top with optional Parmesan cheese.

Kimberley Barber
Byron Center, Michigan

QUICK CASSOULET

Total Servings: 6–8
Preparation Time: 45 minutes
Challenge Level: Easy

"Cassoulet is a traditional French casserole with many regional variations. The name comes from the deep earthenware pot, the cassole, in which it is traditionally cooked."

Preparation at Camp:

1. Sauté sausage, onion, and garlic in oil in cook pot over medium heat.

2. Add carrots, tomatoes, thyme, and bay leaf to the pot.

3. Heat to boiling then add beans and chicken, including chicken juice, to the pot.

4. Reduce heat to a simmer and cook until carrots are tender, about 20 minutes.

5. Serve with crushed crackers as a topping.

Ken Harbison
Rochester, New York

8 ounces smoked sausage, sliced into chunks

1 medium-size onion, chopped

2 cloves garlic, minced

1 teaspoon olive oil

4 medium-size carrots, cut into 1-inch pieces

1 (14.5-ounce) can low-sodium diced tomatoes, undrained

1 teaspoon dried thyme

1 small bay leaf

2 (15.5-ounce) cans cannellini beans, drained and rinsed

1 (12.5-ounce) can water-packed premium chicken, undrained

16 Ritz Crackers, crushed

Required Equipment:
Medium-size cook pot

PORCUPINE SOUP

Total Servings: 6–8
Preparation Time: 45 minutes
Challenge Level: Easy

"This is a simple recipe that children love to prepare. The meatballs really look like small porcupines!"

1 pound lean ground beef

1 medium onion, chopped

1 cup Minute Rice

¼ teaspoon salt

1 egg

2 (10.75-ounce) cans condensed tomato soup

2 (10.75-ounce) cans water (use empty soup can to measure)

Optional: shredded cheese, croutons

Required Equipment:
Medium-size mixing bowl

Medium-size cook pot

Preparation at Camp:

1. Combine beef, onion, rice, salt, and egg in a bowl.

2. Gently knead meat mixture to combine ingredients, then form into small, bite-size balls.

3. In a cook pot, combine tomato soup and water and bring to a boil.

4. Immediately reduce heat to a simmer, then gently drop beef balls into the soup.

5. Cover pot and cook for about 30 minutes, until meatballs are cooked through.

6. Serve with optional shredded cheese and croutons.

Kathleen Kirby
Milltown, New Jersey

CHICKEN COUNTRY CAPTAIN

Total Servings: 6–8
Preparation Time: 45 minutes
Challenge Level: Moderate

"Chicken Country Captain is thought to have been brought to Savannah, Georgia, in the early 1800s by a British sea captain who had been stationed in Bengali, India. It was a favorite dish of Franklin D. Roosevelt, served at his Georgia cottage."

Preparation at Camp:

1. Sauté chicken in oil in a cook pot over medium heat until browned on all sides.

2. Remove chicken from pot, then sauté onion and bell pepper in the same pot until softened.

3. Return browned chicken to the pot and add garlic, diced tomatoes with juice, curry powder, thyme, and raisins, then bring to a boil.

4. Reduce heat to a simmer and continue to cook until chicken is tender, about 20 minutes.

5. While chicken simmers, cook rice in 3 cups water in a second pot for about 20 minutes, until water is absorbed.

6. Serve chicken over rice, garnished with almonds and optional chutney.

Ken Harbison
Rochester, New York

4 boneless chicken breasts, chopped into ³/₄-inch chunks

2 tablespoons olive oil

1 large onion, coarsely chopped

1 green bell pepper, cut into 1-inch pieces

2 cloves garlic, minced

1 (14.5-ounce) can diced tomatoes, undrained

2 teaspoons curry powder

¹/₂ teaspoon dried thyme

¹/₃ cup raisins

1¹/₂ cups converted rice

3 cups water

¹/₃ cup sliced almonds

Optional: ¹/₂ cup Major Grey's Chutney

Required Equipment:
2 medium-size cook pots

WHITEWATER ALFREDO

Total Servings: 8–10
Preparation Time: 30 minutes
Challenge Level: Moderate

V-LO

"Delicious as is, or served with chicken, shrimp, bacon, garlic, or mushrooms."

1 pound fettuccine pasta

1 cup (2 standard sticks) butter

1 pint heavy whipping cream

2 cups shredded Parmesan cheese

2 tablespoons dried parsley

Salt and ground black pepper to taste

Required Equipment:
Large cook pot

Medium-size frying pan

Preparation at Camp:

1. Boil pasta in cook pot according to package directions. Drain and set aside.

2. Melt butter in a frying pan over low heat.

3. Add cream to pan and bring to a gentle simmer, stirring often.

4. Blend Parmesan cheese into the butter-cream mixture, a little at a time to prevent cheese from clumping.

5. Pour sauce over drained pasta. Toss.

6. Sprinkle pasta with parsley, salt, and black pepper, then serve.

Jason Cagle
Jacksonville, Florida

MAPLE SYRUP SALMON

Total Servings: 3–4
Preparation Time: 15 minutes
Challenge Level: Easy

"This is our favorite way to prepare salmon . . . sweet and delicious!"

Preparation at Camp:

1. Warm oil in a frying pan over medium heat.

2. Carefully place salmon, skin side down, in the pan.

3. Cover fish with maple syrup, juice from squeezed lemon wedges, and pieces of rosemary sprig.

4. Cook salmon on both sides until flesh is opaque and easily separates with a fork.

3 tablespoons olive oil

1 pound salmon fillets with skin

¼ cup maple syrup

1 lemon, cut into wedges

1 sprig fresh rosemary

Required Equipment:
Medium-size frying pan

Christine and Tim Conners
Statesboro, Georgia

BACKYARD RENDEZVOUS KIELBASA

Total Servings: 3–5
Preparation Time: 45 minutes
Challenge Level: Easy

"I've been creating different forms of this recipe at home for many years. Now I prepare it for parties and campouts."

1 (20-ounce) can pineapple chunks, undrained

Water as per step 1 of instructions

3 tablespoons brown sugar

2 tablespoons cornstarch

1 tablespoon butter

14 ounces Polska kielbasa sausage, cut into ¼-inch disks

Optional: 1 (15-ounce) can sweet potatoes, cubed

Required Equipment:
Medium-size frying pan

Preparation at Camp:

1. Pour juice from the can of pineapple, along with whatever additional water is needed to equal 1 cup, into a frying pan.

2. Add brown sugar and cornstarch to the pan and stir well over low heat.

3. Once the sauce thickens, add pineapple chunks, butter, sausage, and optional sweet potatoes. Stir.

4. Cover pan and allow to simmer for at least 30 minutes before serving.

Option: *This recipe goes great over rice.*

Debra Moore
Sutton, Massachusetts

GLACIER BAY GREEN PEPPERS

Total Servings: 4
Preparation Time: 30 minutes
Challenge Level: Easy

Preparation at Camp:

1. Remove tops from green peppers and carefully scoop seeds and webbing from the insides.

2. Mix hash, onion, and cheese together in a bowl.

3. Stuff hash mixture into the peppers, dividing the hash evenly among them.

4. Place peppers on a skillet, tops facing upward. Surround peppers with water to a depth of about 1/4 inch.

5. Cover skillet with a tent of foil and cook over medium heat for 15 to 20 minutes or until the hash is warmed through and the cheese melts.

4 large green bell peppers

1 (15-ounce) can corned beef hash

1 onion, chopped

1 cup shredded cheese (your choice)

Water as per step 4 instructions

Required Equipment:
Small mixing bowl

Medium-size frying pan

Aluminum foil

Christine and Tim Conners
Statesboro, Georgia

TRAIL DRIVE SHRIMP

Total Servings: 4–6
Preparation Time: 30 minutes
Challenge Level: Easy

2 tablespoons sunflower oil

1 onion, sliced

1 red bell pepper, cut into thin strips

1 green bell pepper, cut into thin strips

1 jalapeño pepper, diced

1 bunch fresh cilantro, trimmed and chopped

1 lemon, sliced into large wedges

2 cloves garlic, minced

1 tablespoon dried oregano

Salt and ground black pepper to taste

2 pounds raw shrimp, peeled with tail on

Required Equipment:
Large frying pan

Preparation at Camp:

1. Warm oil in a frying pan over medium heat.

2. Sauté all remaining ingredients, except shrimp, until vegetables are tender.

3. Add shrimp and continue cooking until shrimp turn pink, about 3 minutes.

4. Remove lemon wedges and serve.

Robert Dowdy
Great Falls, Montana

FISHERMAN'S FRY

Total Servings: 6–8
Preparation Time: 30 minutes
Challenge Level: Moderate

Preparation at Camp:

1. Combine Bisquick, beer, eggs, salt, paprika, and garlic powder in a bowl. Mix well to form a dipping batter.

2. Dry fish fillets thoroughly with paper towels to help ensure the batter clings to the fish.

3. Warm 1 cup oil in a frying pan over medium heat. Oil is ready for frying when a small drop of water "pops" when dripped into the pan.

4. Dip both sides of each fillet in the batter.

5. Carefully lay fish side-by-side in the pan. Work in batches to avoid overcrowding.

6. Immediately slide spatula under each fillet to loosen the fish and ensure that it doesn't stick to the pan.

7. Fry fish for about 3 to 5 minutes per side, using more oil when it begins to run low. Serve fish once batter turns a golden brown.

2½ cups Bisquick Heart Smart Pancake and Baking Mix

1 (12-ounce) bottle beer

2 eggs

½ teaspoon salt

½ teaspoon paprika

½ teaspoon garlic powder

2 pounds cleaned white-meat fish fillets

1–2 cups safflower oil

Required Equipment:
Medium-size mixing bowl

Medium-size frying pan

Spatula

Option: Serve fish with coleslaw and tarter sauce to really round out the meal!

*Christine and Tim Conners
Statesboro, Georgia*

SKILLET CHICKEN AND RICE

Total Servings: 6–8
Preparation Time: 45 minutes
Challenge Level: Easy

3 tablespoons butter

1 pound skinless boneless chicken breasts, chopped into bite-size pieces

1 (7.2-ounce) package chicken flavor Rice-a-Roni

1 (14.5-ounce) can chicken broth

1 (14.5-ounce) can water (use empty broth can to measure)

4 carrots, peeled and sliced into thin disks

4 stalks celery, chopped

1 onion, diced

Required Equipment:
Large frying pan

Preparation at Camp:

1. Melt butter over medium heat in a frying pan.

2. Lightly brown the chicken, then add the rice-pasta mixture from the Rice-a-Roni package to pan. Reserve the seasoning from the package.

3. Stir in chicken broth and water.

4. Add carrots, celery, onion, and seasoning from the Rice-a-Roni package to the pan. Stir well and bring liquid to a boil.

5. Reduce heat to a simmer and continue to cook for about 20 minutes, until chicken is cooked through and rice-pasta is plump.

Guy Wills
Niceville, Florida

SKY RIVER SKILLET SPAGHETTI

Total Servings: 8–10
Preparation Time: 30 minutes
Challenge Level: Easy

"The beauty of this recipe is that it can be prepared using just a skillet."

Preparation at Camp:

1. In a large frying pan, brown beef with onions, garlic, and mushrooms. Carefully drain excess liquid.

2. To the pan, add tomato sauce, water, tomato paste, chili powder, Italian seasoning, sugar, and salt.

3. Stir well, bring to a boil, then reduce heat to a simmer.

4. Break spaghetti noodles in half and add to the pan. Stir to separate and coat noodles.

5. Cover pan and continue to simmer, stirring occasionally, for about 15 minutes or until noodles are al dente. While the noodles are cooking, add additional water, a little at a time, if needed.

6. Top spaghetti with optional Parmesan cheese and serve.

> This dish can also be cooked in a Dutch oven over coals.

Christine and Tim Conners
Statesboro, Georgia

1 pound lean ground beef

2 onions, diced

4 cloves garlic, minced

8 ounces fresh mushrooms, sliced

2 (15-ounce) cans tomato sauce

1 (15-ounce) can water (use empty tomato sauce can to measure)

1 (6-ounce) can tomato paste

1 tablespoon chili powder

2 tablespoon Italian seasoning

2 tablespoons granulated sugar

2 teaspoons salt

½ pound thin spaghetti noodles

Optional: grated Parmesan cheese to taste

Required Equipment:
Large frying pan

SEVEN HILLS CHILI

Total Servings: 8
Preparation Time: 1½ hours
Challenge Level: Moderate

"I tested and retested this recipe for five years and ended up with some sort of Western Rockies–Cincinnati Hills concoction. Boy, it sure is good. I use all-organic ingredients, which I think makes the flavor even better."

2 pounds ground venison, elk, or buffalo

1 medium onion, finely chopped

2 tablespoons sunflower oil

2 tablespoons tomato paste

1 (28-ounce) can crushed tomatoes

1 green bell pepper, diced

2 cloves garlic, minced

2 tablespoons ground cumin

½ teaspoon sea salt

½ teaspoon fresh-cracked black pepper

1 teaspoon dried oregano

2 dried bay leaves

1 tablespoon chili powder

½ teaspoon ground cayenne pepper

2 tablespoons cocoa powder

½ teaspoon ground cinnamon

1 (15-ounce) can kidney beans, drained and rinsed

1 (15-ounce) can black beans, drained and rinsed

Required Equipment:
Large frying pan

Preparation at Camp:

1. In a large frying pan over medium heat, sauté meat with onion in oil for about 15 minutes.

2. Add remaining ingredients, except the beans. Simmer on medium-high heat for about 30 minutes.

3. Reduce heat to low, add beans, and simmer for an additional 30 minutes before serving.

John Bostick
Cincinnati, Ohio

HOBO BURGERS

Total Servings: 4
Preparation Time: 45 minutes
Challenge Level: Easy

"Mawmaw, my grandmother, taught me this recipe. She recalled that, during the Great Depression, the homeless would prepare a similar dish by finding a little meat and a few vegetables then tossing them together to make a meal fit for king."

Preparation at Camp:

1. Form 4 hamburger patties from the ground beef. Set each patty on its own piece of foil.

2. Place potato and onion slices, along with any optional vegetables, on top of the hamburger patties. Season with garlic salt and Mrs. Dash to taste.

3. Loosely wrap hamburger and vegetables in the foil while sealing edges tightly.

4. Place burger packets on a grate low over the embers of the campfire and cook for 15 to 30 minutes. Occasionally rotate packets. Burgers are ready to serve once the internal temperature of the patties reaches 160°F.

5. Carefully remove and open packets, avoiding escaping steam.

6. Place each patty on hamburger bun with optional cheese and burger toppings. Enjoy the cooked vegetables as a side or on the burger.

1 pound ground beef

1 medium potato, thinly sliced

1 medium onion, thinly sliced

Optional: chopped celery, carrots, bell peppers, cabbage

Garlic salt and Mrs. Dash to taste

4 hamburger buns

Optional: cheese, lettuce, tomato slices, ketchup

Required Equipment:
Heavy-duty aluminum foil

Hobo Burgers can be prepared ahead of time, then stored in a cooler until ready to cook. Foil packs can also be heated on the grill.

Tina Welch
Harper, Kansas

CHEESY BACON CHICKEN

Total Servings: 4
Preparation Time: 45 minutes
Challenge Level: Easy

"This recipe can be scaled so easily: for just a few people or a whole group of campers. Goes great with broccoli and rice!"

4 boneless chicken breasts

4 slices bacon

4 slices mozzarella cheese

Required Equipment:
Heavy-duty aluminum foil

Preparation at Camp:

1. Pound chicken breasts for uniform thickness and even cooking.

2. Cut each slice of bacon in half for 8 pieces total.

3. In the middle of each of 4 large squares of foil, place 2 pieces bacon. On each pair of bacon pieces, set a chicken breast.

4. Fold foil over the chicken to create a tightly sealed pouch.

5. Cook chicken on a grate over the campfire for about 20 to 30 minutes, flipping the foil pouch about halfway through. Chicken is ready to be removed from heat once the internal temperature reaches 165°F.

6. Top each breast with a slice of mozzarella then serve.

Oralia Lopez
Royse City, Texas

OSCEOLA SALMON

Total Servings: 4
Preparation Time: 45 minutes
Challenge Level: Moderate

"I prepared this recipe for the first time while camping in the Osceola National Forest in Florida. I wrapped the salmon in foil and cooked it on a makeshift grill over embers from the campfire."

Preparation at Camp:

1. In a small bowl, whip Worcestershire sauce, granulated garlic, granulated onion, and minced fresh garlic with softened butter.

2. Spread half of the butter rub on a large sheet of foil over an area about the size of the 4 salmon fillets.

3. Lay fillets, skin side down and side-by-side, on the butter rub, then coat top side of fillets with remainder of the rub.

4. Lay two basil leaves over each fillet.

5. Form a pouch around the fillets with the foil, using a second sheet over the top if necessary. Seal foil tightly around the edges.

6. Place foil pouch on a grate over the campfire.

7. Bake for about 20 to 30 minutes. Fish is ready once it flakes easily with a fork.

8. Carefully remove foil pack from fire. Reserve juices from the foil.

9. Serve, pouring reserved juices over fillets and lightly sprinkling with cayenne pepper to taste.

2 tablespoons Worcestershire sauce

1 tablespoon granulated garlic

1 tablespoon granulated onion

4 tablespoons minced fresh garlic

1/2 cup (1 standard stick) butter, softened

4 (8-ounce) salmon fillets

8 whole leaves fresh basil

Ground cayenne pepper to taste

Required Equipment:
Small mixing bowl

Heavy-duty aluminum foil

Jason Cagle
Jacksonville, Florida

ONION BOMBS

Total Servings: 4–8
Preparation Time: 45 minutes
Challenge Level: Moderate

4 very large onions

1 pound lean ground beef

½ cup quick oats

¼ teaspoon garlic powder

Salt, ground black pepper, and cayenne pepper to taste

1 tablespoon Worcestershire sauce

1 egg

Required Equipment:
Medium-size mixing bowl

Heavy-duty aluminum foil

Preparation at Camp:

1. Cut each onion in half.

2. Remove outer skin layer as well as the center from each onion, leaving 2 or 3 thick layers that create a half-shell bowl.

3. Dice some of the excess onion pieces to fill ¼ cup.

4. Combine ground beef, oats, seasonings, Worcestershire sauce, egg, and diced onion in a mixing bowl. Gently knead mixture.

5. Divide meat mixture among the 8 onion half-shells.

6. Reassemble each onion by aligning the cut layers from 2 halves. Wrap each of the 4 onion balls with a large sheet of foil.

7. Bake directly on hot coals for about 30 minutes, until meat is thoroughly cooked to at least 160°F. Occasionally rotate the foil balls while roasting.

Option: Your favorite ingredients can be combined to create a tailored meat mixture. Consider bread crumbs, crackers, diced bell peppers, or minced garlic.

> Hot fires work best with this recipe, as the outer onion layers will better caramelize and sweeten the meat mixture.

Cal Beard
Cedar Hill, Texas

HULI-HULI CHICKEN

Total Servings: 4
Preparation Time: 15 minutes
Challenge Level: Easy

"This form of barbecued chicken is very popular in Hawaii and often sold in large quantities at fundraisers. The name means 'turn-turn' in Hawaiian and refers to the calls the cooks make as they rotate racks of chickens over large grills."

Preparation at Camp:

1. Combine soy sauce, brown sugar, ketchup, juice concentrate, garlic, and ginger in a small bowl and mix well.

2. Barbecue chicken on high heat, turning every 5 minutes or so and basting with the sauce.

3. Continue turning and basting until chicken reaches an internal temperature of 165°F.

Ken Harbison
Rochester, New York

¼ cup soy sauce

2 tablespoons brown sugar

2 tablespoons ketchup

2 tablespoons frozen pineapple juice concentrate

2 teaspoons chopped garlic

1 tablespoon minced fresh ginger

4 chicken quarters or boneless chicken breasts

Required Equipment:
Small mixing bowl

WORLD TRAVELER FOIL PACKETS

Total Servings: 8
Preparation Time: 45 minutes
Challenge Level: Moderate

"You'll find a world of flavors in this recipe. Experiment with the ingredients—the combinations are endless!"

Mediterranean Packs:
½ cup olive oil

2 pounds skinless boneless chicken breasts, cut into thin strips

4 new potatoes, cut into thin wedges

1 red onion, cut into thin rings

4 ounces pitted Kalamata olives

8 cloves garlic, minced

1 (14-ounce) can quartered artichoke hearts, drained

½ cup balsamic vinegar

6 ounces crumbled Feta cheese

Asian Packs:
½ cup peanut oil

2 pounds raw peeled shrimp or extra-firm tofu

1 (11.8-ounce) jar Kikkoman Teriyaki Baste and Glaze

1 bell pepper, cut into thin slices

1 (6-ounce) package sliced almonds

1 head bok choy, trimmed and chopped

1 sweet onion, cut into thin wedges

½ pound snow peas

1 (20-ounce) can crushed pineapple in heavy syrup, undrained

1 head broccoli, cut into quartered florets

Bavarian Packs:
2 pounds smoked brats

1 (15-ounce) can butter beans, drained and rinsed

2 small summer squash, cut into thin slices

2 tart green apples, cored and cut into thin wedges

1 (14-ounce) can sauerkraut, drained

1 (10-ounce) bottle prepared mustard

Central American Packs:
2 pounds lean ground beef, formed into 8 thin patties

2 (15-ounce) cans black beans, drained and rinsed

1 (11-ounce) can Mexicorn-style corn, drained

1 (16-ounce) jar salsa

2 cups shredded Mexican-style cheese

1 (16-ounce) container sour cream (added after cooking)

Optional: 8 tortillas (for serving with cooked ingredients)

Required Equipment:
Heavy-duty aluminum foil (18 inches wide)

Preparation at Camp:
1. Choose 1 of the 4 international foil pack options.
2. On each of 8 (18 x 18-inch) sheets of foil, layer ingredients in the order listed.
3. Form a loose pouch around the ingredients, then seal very tightly by repeatedly folding the edges over. Attempt to make the packets airtight.
4. If packets have been customized for each camper, put a name on each packet with a marker.
5. Heat packet on a grate over a campfire or grill for about 20 minutes. Check meats for proper cooking temperature before serving, 165°F being a safe target.

Foil cooking may appear simple, but it can be challenging to balance fully cooked meat with tender vegetables. The following tips will help ensure consistently great results:

• When using uncooked meat, place it at the bottom of the packet, closest to the heat source.

• It is crucial to the cooking process that the packs are sealed tightly to trap steam. A packet that loses too much moisture will cook unevenly or char.

• Do not place packets over intense heat, which will burn the contents. Instead, cook packets over a low campfire or on a grill at medium heat, never in direct contact with the flames.

Christine and Tim Conners
Statesboro, Georgia

PUYALLUP PLANKED SALMON

Total Servings: 1
Preparation Time: 30 minutes
Challenge Level: Moderate

"Long ago, the Puyallup natives of the Northwest taught Europeans how to cook fish on sticks or planks, instead of boiling it. This remains a popular cooking method in the area."

½ pound salmon fillet or steak

½ teaspoon olive oil

½ teaspoon powdered jerk or Cajun seasoning

Required Equipment:
Untreated cedar wood shingle or plank, washed then soaked in water for about an hour

Aluminum steam table pan, if grill has no lid

Preparation at Camp:

1. Prepare salmon by lightly rubbing both sides with olive oil, then heavily sprinkling one side with seasoning. Add seasoning to the skinless side if using fillets.

2. Heat one side of the plank or shingle over a flame or coals until it smokes lightly, about 3 minutes.

3. Remove plank from the grill using tongs, turn hot side up, and immediately place salmon on browned side of the wood, with the seasoned side of the fish facing up. If using fillets, the skin side should be placed on the wood, with the thickest part of the fillet on the thinnest end of the shingle.

4. Immediately return plank to the grill and cover with lid. If grill does not have a lid, an aluminum steam table pan can be placed upside down over the fish. The pan reflects heat back on the top of the fish, allowing it to bake.

5. Cook until the fish meat is opaque and easily flakes with a fork. As an example, about 10 minutes is required for a 1-inch-thick fillet cooked over high heat. If using a thermometer, cook until internal temperature is at least 145°F.

Ken and Judy Harbison
Rochester, New York

If the plank catches fire, carefully spray wood with water to douse, being careful to stay far enough away from the flames to avoid flare-up. Lower the grill temperature to prevent reoccurrence.

Be certain the wood has not been treated with preservatives. If shingles are not available, planks may be cut into 10- to 12-inch lengths from 1 x 6 cedar lumber. Do not use other types of wood, such as pine, which will impart a turpentine flavor to your fish. Prepackaged cedar grilling planks can be found at larger retail stores.

Photo by Scott Simerly

HOOSIER'S GRILLED DUCK BREASTS

Total Servings: 4
Preparation Time: 30 minutes
(plus about 4 hours for marinating)
Challenge Level: Easy

"Years ago, I had the opportunity to tour Maple Leaf Farms, located in northern Indiana, one of the largest duck producers in America. Their whole ducks are delicious, but their boneless duck breasts are exceptionally meaty. I once cooked them on the grill, and my brother-in-law was convinced I was serving beef filet mignon."

Marinade:
½ cup olive oil

¼ cup fresh lemon juice

1 teaspoon dried Greek oregano

½ teaspoon ground thyme

¼ cup minced fresh parsley

½ teaspoon salt

¼ teaspoon fresh-cracked black pepper

4 skin-on boneless duck breasts

Required Equipment:
Gallon-size heavy-duty ziplock bag

Preparation at Camp:

1. Combine marinade ingredients in a gallon-size heavy-duty ziplock bag. Place duck breasts in bag.

2. Seal ziplock bag tightly, shake to coat, then place the bag in a cooler for at least 4 hours to marinate.

3. To prevent cross contamination, discard the marinade at this time. It isn't needed anyway because the duck breasts self-baste on the grill.

4. Grill breasts over medium heat, skin side down, for 10 minutes, then flip and cook on the opposite side until meat is cooked through to 165°F, about 10 more minutes.

5. Remove breasts from grill, allow to rest and cool for a few minutes, then slice at an angle into ½-inch-thick medallions before serving.

John Bostick
Cincinnati, Ohio

SOUTHWEST SAUSAGE KABOBS

Total Servings: 4
Preparation Time: 1 hour
Challenge Level: Easy

Preparation at Camp:

1. Combine honey, lime juice, chipotle pepper, and cilantro in a gallon-size ziplock bag.

2. Add bell pepper, onion, cherry tomatoes, and smoked sausage to the bag.

3. Seal bag tightly, shake to coat the vegetables and sausage, then place bag in a cooler for about 30 minutes to allow ingredients to marinate.

4. Alternating between vegetables and sausage, thread onto 4 skewers.

5. Set kabobs on the grill over medium heat. Cook for 10 to 15 minutes, rotating periodically.

Christine and Tim Conners
Statesboro, Georgia

½ cup honey

½ cup lime juice

1 teaspoon ground chipotle pepper

1 teaspoon dried cilantro

1 red bell pepper, cut into wedges

1 sweet onion, cut into wedges

1 pint cherry tomatoes

1 (14-ounce) package smoked sausage, cut into 1-inch pieces

Required Equipment:
Gallon-size ziplock bag

4 metal skewers

ROGUE RIVER SHORT RIBS

Total Servings: 4–6
Preparation Time: 30 minutes
(plus about 2 hours for marinating)
Challenge Level: Easy

½ cup teriyaki sauce

¼ cup orange marmalade

2½ pounds short ribs, trimmed of fat

Required Equipment:
Medium-size mixing bowl

Preparation at Camp:

1. Combine teriyaki sauce and marmalade in a bowl. Stir well.

2. Add ribs to the bowl and coat in the marinade sauce.

3. Cover bowl tightly and set in a cooler for about 2 hours to marinate, rotating ribs occasionally to recoat.

4. Cook ribs on a grill over medium heat, turning occasionally.

5. Remove ribs from grill and serve once internal temperature reaches at least 145°F.

Christine and Tim Conners
Statesboro, Georgia

VEGETABLE KEBABS

Total Servings: 4–6
Preparation Time: 30 minutes
Challenge Level: Moderate

Preparation at Camp:

1. Pare eggplant and cut into 1-inch cubes. Immediately baste eggplant with Italian salad dressing in bowl to prevent browning.

2. Cut pineapple rings into eighths. Chop all other ingredients, except tomatoes, into 1-inch pieces.

3. Thread all ingredients in alternating order onto each skewer.

4. Lay loaded skewers on a large sheet of foil and drizzle with some of the dressing from the bowl.

5. Place skewers on a hot grill. Turn every few minutes, drizzling with remaining marinade.

6. Kebabs will be ready to serve once vegetables become slightly tender, about 6 to 10 minutes after placing on the grill.

Option: You can substitute teriyaki sauce for the Italian salad dressing.

8 ounces eggplant

½ cup zesty Italian salad dressing

8 ounces fresh or canned pineapple rings

1 large green bell pepper

1 red or yellow bell pepper

1 sweet onion

8 ounces fresh mushrooms

1 small yellow summer squash

1 small zucchini

8 ounces firm tofu

8 ounces cherry tomatoes

Required Equipment:
Small mixing bowl

12 (1-foot) skewers

Heavy-duty aluminum foil

If using wooden skewers, soak in water for at least a half hour before using. Otherwise the skewers may catch fire while cooking.

Ken Harbison
Rochester, New York

HAWAIIAN KEBABS

Total Servings: 4–6
Preparation Time: 30 minutes
(plus about 1 hour for marinating)
Challenge Level: Moderate

1 (20-ounce) can pineapple rings

½ cup teriyaki sauce

2 tablespoons sesame oil

1 teaspoon fresh grated ginger

1 teaspoon honey

1½ pounds boneless tenderloin or center-cut pork

1 large green bell pepper

1 red bell pepper

1 sweet onion

Required Equipment:
Small mixing bowl

2 quart-size ziplock freezer bags

12 (1-foot) skewers

Heavy-duty aluminum foil

Preparation at Camp:

1. Drain pineapple, reserving the juice.

2. Prepare marinade by mixing ½ cup reserved pineapple juice with teriyaki sauce, oil, ginger, and honey in a bowl.

3. Chop meat into 1-inch cubes, trimming fat, then place meat cubes in a quart-size ziplock bag with half of the marinade. Tightly seal bag and shake to coat meat.

4. Reserve the other half of the marinade in a separate ziplock bag. Place both bags in a cooler and allow meat to marinate for about an hour.

5. Once it's time for dinner, drain and discard marinade from the bag containing the meat. Be careful not to cross contaminate the marinade in the other bag!

6. Cut pineapple rings into eighths.

7. Chop bell peppers into 1-inch squares, discarding ribs and seeds.

8. Peel onion and chop into 1-inch pieces, each a couple of layers thick.

9. Thread meat and vegetables in alternating order onto each skewer.

10. Lay loaded skewers on a large sheet of foil and drizzle with some of the reserved marinade.

11. Place skewers on a hot grill. Turn every few minutes and occasionally drizzle with remaining marinade.

12. Kebabs will be ready to serve once the internal temperature of the pork reaches at least 145°F, about 10 to 20 minutes after placing on the grill.

Option: *You can substitute four boneless chicken breasts for the pork and raise the target cooking temperature to 165°F.*

If using wooden skewers, soak in water for at least a half hour before using. Otherwise, the skewers may catch fire while cooking.

Ken Harbison
Rochester, New York

SHISH KEBABS

Total Servings: 4–6
Preparation Time: 30 minutes
(plus about 2 hours for marinating)
Challenge Level: Moderate

"Meat and vegetables have been grilled on skewers in Greece and the Near East since antiquity."

1 teaspoon ground cumin

½ teaspoon ground coriander

¼ teaspoon ground cayenne pepper or 2 teaspoons red curry powder

1½ pounds tender beef, such as top sirloin or leg of lamb

½ cup fresh lemon juice

¼ cup olive oil

½ teaspoon salt

1 pound eggplant

1 large green bell pepper

1 sweet onion

Required Equipment:
Drinking cup

Small mixing bowl

2 quart-size ziplock freezer bags

12 (1-foot) skewers

Heavy-duty aluminum foil

Preparation at Camp:

1. Combine cumin, coriander, and cayenne or curry in a drinking cup and rub the spice blend on the meat.

2. Prepare the marinade sauce by blending lemon juice, oil, and salt in a small bowl.

3. Chop meat into 1-inch cubes, trimming fat, then place cubes in a quart-size ziplock bag with half the marinade. Tightly seal bag and shake to coat meat.

4. Reserve the other half of the marinade in a separate ziplock bag. Place both bags in a cooler and allow meat to marinate for about 2 hours, but no longer.

5. Once it's time for dinner, drain and discard marinade from the bag containing the meat. Be careful not to cross contaminate the marinade in the other bag!

6. Pare eggplant and cut into 1-inch cubes. Immediately baste eggplant with a little of the reserved marinade in small bowl to prevent browning.

7. Chop bell pepper into 1-inch squares, discarding ribs and seeds.

8. Peel onion and chop into 1-inch pieces, each a couple of layers thick.

9. Thread meat and vegetables in alternating order onto each skewer.

10. Lay loaded skewers on a large sheet of foil and drizzle with some of the reserved marinade.

11. Place skewers on a hot grill. Turn every few minutes and occasionally drizzle with remaining marinade.

12. Kebabs will be ready to serve once the internal temperature of the meat reaches at least 145°F, about 10 to 20 minutes after placing on the grill.

Option: Serve the cooked kebabs with rice or pitas.

If using wooden skewers, soak in water for at least a half hour before using. Otherwise the skewers may catch fire while cooking. Do not marinate meat with acidic sauces, such as the one used in this recipe, for more than 2 hours. Otherwise the surface of the meat can become mushy then dry out during cooking.

Ken Harbison
Rochester, New York

SHASHLIK

Total Servings: 4–6
Preparation Time: 30 minutes
(plus about 3 hours for marinating)
Challenge Level: Moderate

"Shashlik and related kebab recipes are popular in eastern Europe and Russia. Meat, originally lamb but now also beef or pork, is usually marinated with wine and herbs. It may be served plain or with pitas, rice, or salad."

½ cup red wine

¼ cup olive oil

1 clove garlic, minced

½ teaspoon ground oregano

2 dried bay leaves

1 tablespoon Worcestershire sauce

½ teaspoon salt

1½ pounds tender beef, such as top sirloin or leg of lamb

1 large green bell pepper

1 sweet onion

8 ounces small mushrooms

12 cherry tomatoes

Required Equipment:
Small mixing bowl

2 quart-size ziplock freezer bags

12 (1-foot) skewers

Heavy-duty aluminum foil

Preparation at Camp:

1. Prepare marinade by blending wine, oil, garlic, oregano, bay leaves, Worcestershire sauce, and salt in a small bowl.

2. Chop meat into 1-inch cubes and place in a quart-size ziplock bag with half of the marinade and 1 of the bay leaves. Tightly seal bag and shake to coat meat.

3. Reserve other half of the marinade, along with the second bay leaf, in a separate ziplock bag. Place both bags in a cooler and allow meat to marinate for at least 3 hours.

4. Once it's time for dinner, drain and discard marinade from the bag containing the meat. Be careful not to cross contaminate the marinade in the other bag!

5. Chop bell pepper into 1-inch squares, discarding ribs and seeds.

6. Peel the onion and chop it into 1-inch pieces, each a couple of layers thick.

7. Thread meat, peppers, onion, mushrooms, and tomatoes in alternating order onto each skewer, finishing with a tomato on the end of each to give a nice presentation.

8. Lay loaded skewers on a large sheet of foil and drizzle with some of the reserved marinade.

9. Place skewers on hot grill. Turn every few minutes and occasionally drizzle with remaining marinade.

10. Kebabs will be ready to serve once the internal temperature of the meat reaches at least 145°F, about 10 to 20 minutes after placing on the grill.

Options: *You can substitute pomegranate juice for the red wine.*

Serve the cooked kebabs stuffed into pita halves.

If using wooden skewers, soak in water for at least a half hour before using. Otherwise the skewers may catch fire while cooking.

Ken Harbison
Rochester, New York

Side Dishes

PIEDMONT POTATO WEDGES

V-LO

Total Servings: 4–6
Preparation Time: 1 hour
Challenge Level: Easy

"I received this recipe from a coworker and converted the cooking instructions to make it Dutch oven–friendly. Anything cooked in an electric oven indoors can be cooked outdoors in a Dutch oven!"

Preparation at Camp:

1. Combine flour, Parmesan cheese, garlic salt, onion salt, chili powder, and black pepper in a gallon-size ziplock bag.

2. Add potato wedges, 4 or 5 at a time, to the bag. Seal bag and shake to coat the wedges, repeating until all wedges are coated.

3. Melt butter in a Dutch oven over 21 coals and carefully lay the potato wedges into the oven. Place lid on the oven.

4. Bake potatoes for 15 minutes using 14 coals on the lid and 7 under the oven.

5. Flip potatoes and cook for another 15 minutes, or until potatoes are tender.

Paul Vanover
Morganton, North Carolina

¼ cup all-purpose flour

¼ cup grated Parmesan cheese

¼ teaspoon garlic salt

¼ teaspoon onion salt

¼ teaspoon chili powder

½ teaspoon ground black pepper

3 large potatoes, skin on, washed, and cut into wedges

¼ cup (½ standard stick) butter

Required Equipment:

Gallon-size ziplock bag

10-inch camp Dutch oven

Photo licensed by Shutterstock.com

CHILLY NIGHTS CRAB DIP

Total Servings: 6–8
Preparation Time: 1 hour
Challenge Level: Easy

1 pound lump crabmeat

1 clove garlic, minced

1/4 cup chopped
jalapeño peppers

4 ounces shredded
Monterey Jack cheese

1/2 cup mayonnaise

2 teaspoons
Worcestershire sauce

1 teaspoon hot sauce

1/2 teaspoon salt

1/4 cup shredded
Parmesan cheese

Tortilla chips or crackers

Required Equipment:
Medium-size mixing
bowl

10-inch camp Dutch
oven

Preparation at Camp:

1. In a bowl, combine crabmeat, garlic, jalapeños, Jack cheese, mayonnaise, Worcestershire, hot sauce, and salt. Mix well.

2. Transfer crab mixture to a Dutch oven. Top with Parmesan cheese. Place lid on the oven.

3. Using 14 coals on the lid and 7 under the oven, bake for about 30 minutes, until the top of the dip is golden brown and bubbly.

4. Remove from coals and allow to rest for about 5 minutes before serving with tortilla chips or crackers.

Carl Laub
Arlington Heights, Illinois

SNOW BUCK'S CORN PUDDING

Total Servings: 6–8
Preparation Time: 1¼ hours
Challenge Level: Easy

Preparation at Camp:

1. Combine all ingredients in a bowl. Stir well.

2. Pour batter into a greased 9-inch-round baking pan.

3. Set pan on a trivet in the Dutch oven. Place lid on the oven.

4. Using 17 coals on the lid and 8 under the oven, bake for about 50 minutes, until top of the corn pudding becomes golden brown.

Option: Although a drier crumb is likely to result, you can pour the batter directly into the smaller 10-inch Dutch oven, lined with greased aluminum foil. Bake for the same period of time, but use a total of 21 coals, with 14 on the lid and 7 under the oven. Pay close attention toward the end of baking to be sure the pudding doesn't become too dry.

½ cup (1 standard stick) butter, softened

1 (15-ounce) can cream-style corn

1 (15-ounce) can whole kernel corn, undrained

2 eggs, beaten

8 ounces sour cream

1 (8.5-ounce) package Jiffy corn muffin mix

Required Equipment:
Medium-size mixing bowl

9-inch-round baking pan

12-inch camp Dutch oven with trivet

The 12-inch camp Dutch oven is often too spacious when cooking for groups smaller than about 8 people. But there are two important exceptions to this rule: 1) when roasting whole birds or larger cuts of meat, and 2) when baking sensitive foods that call for the use of a pan or rack set on a trivet. This recipe conforms to the latter and needs the width of the 12-inch oven to fit the required pan size.

Ray "Snow Buck" McCune
Fort Wayne, Indiana

RANCH BEANS

Total Servings: 6–8
Preparation Time: 1½ hours
Challenge Level: Easy

1 pound lean ground
beef

1 (28-ounce) can
meatless beans in
tomato sauce

1 (8-ounce) can tomato
sauce

½ green bell pepper,
chopped

2 stalks celery, chopped

1 onion, chopped

2 tablespoons brown
sugar

1 tablespoon prepared
yellow mustard

Required Equipment:
10-inch camp Dutch
oven

Preparation at Camp:

1. In a Dutch oven over 21 coals, brown
   ground beef until no pink remains. Drain
   excess grease.

2. Add remaining ingredients to the cooked
   beef, then stir.

3. Simmer for about an hour, reducing or
   adding coals as needed to control heat. Do
   not allow beans to boil vigorously.

Debra Moore
Sutton, Massachusetts

POTAWATOMI HOT POTATO SALAD

Total Servings: 6–8
Preparation Time: 1½ hours
Challenge Level: Moderate

Preparation at Camp:

1. Boil whole potatoes in a cook pot until spuds easily split with a fork.

2. While potatoes are boiling, fry bacon in a Dutch oven over 18 coals.

3. Remove bacon from Dutch oven, crumble, and set aside.

4. Add onions and celery to the hot bacon grease in Dutch oven. Sauté until onions become translucent.

5. Remove Dutch oven from coals, carefully drain grease from the oven, then transfer cooked onion and celery to a bowl.

6. Peel cooked potatoes and cut into bite-size cubes. Place in bowl containing the onion and celery.

7. Add Miracle Whip, crumbled cooked bacon, olives, salt, and black pepper to the bowl. Top with three-quarters of the cheese and gently mix.

8. Pour potato salad into Dutch oven to a uniform depth.

9. Cover oven and transfer 12 coals to the lid. Bake for about 30 minutes, until potato salad is bubbling hot, refreshing coals as needed.

10. Remove oven from coals and sprinkle remainder of the cheese over the salad. Replace lid and let rest a few minutes while cheese melts before serving.

3 large potatoes

½ pound bacon

1 small onion, diced

1 stalk celery, diced

¾ cup Miracle Whip dressing

2 tablespoons chopped green olives with pimento

1 dash salt

¼ teaspoon ground black pepper

1 cup shredded mild cheddar cheese

Required Equipment:
Medium-size cook pot

10-inch camp Dutch oven

Medium-size mixing bowl

Beth Ann Ast
Michigan City, Indiana

SPIKE'S FUNERAL POTATOES

Total Servings: 6–8
Preparation Time: 1³/₄ hours
Challenge Level: Easy

"This recipe comes from WGN radio's morning host, Spike O'Dell. It's delicious!"

½ cup (1 standard stick) butter, softened

1 (10.75-ounce) can condensed cream of chicken soup

1 cup sour cream

8 ounces shredded cheddar cheese

1 (28-ounce) package frozen Ore-Ida Potatoes O'Brien, thawed

Salt and ground black pepper to taste

Preparation at Camp:

1. Stir butter and soup together in a bowl.

2. Add sour cream, cheese, and potatoes to the bowl and mix well.

3. Transfer potato mixture to a Dutch oven and spread to uniform depth. Place lid on oven.

4. Using 14 coals on the lid and 7 under the oven, bake for 75 minutes, refreshing coals as needed.

5. Remove Dutch oven from coals, let rest for 10 minutes, then serve potatoes with salt and black pepper to taste.

Required Equipment:
Large mixing bowl

10-inch camp Dutch oven

Delano LaGow
Oswego, Illinois

NORTH WOODS CHILI DIP

Total Servings: 8
Preparation Time: 45 minutes
Challenge Level: Easy

Preparation at Camp:
1. Layer cream cheese, chili, green chilies, olives, onion, and jalapeños in a Dutch oven. Cover all with cheddar cheese. Place lid on the oven.

2. Using 14 coals on the lid and 7 under the oven, bake for 25 to 30 minutes, until cheese is fully melted.

3. Serve dip with tortilla or corn chips.

Carl Laub
Arlington Heights, Illinois

8 ounces cream cheese, softened

1 (16-ounce) can no-bean chili

1 (4-ounce) can chopped green chilies

1 (4.25-ounce) can chopped black olives, drained

1 small onion, chopped

2 jalapeños, diced

1 cup shredded sharp cheddar cheese

1 (16-ounce) package tortilla or corn chips

Required Equipment:
10-inch camp Dutch oven

LITTLE MIAMI ONION RINGS

Total Servings: 2
Preparation Time: 30 minutes
Challenge Level: Moderate

V

1 cup sunflower oil

1 large sweet onion

1 cup water

1 cup all-purpose flour

1 teaspoon salt

1/2 teaspoon ground
black pepper

Required Equipment:
Medium-size frying pan

2 bowls, each about 5
inches wide

Paper towels

Preparation at Camp:

1. Warm oil in a frying pan over medium heat.

2. Slice onion into 1/2-inch disks, then break disks apart into rings.

3. Pour 1 cup water into one bowl, and flour, salt, and black pepper into the other bowl. Stir the flour mixture.

4. Working in small batches so as not to overcrowd the pan, dip onion rings, one at a time, into water in the first bowl, then into flour mixture in the second bowl, completely covering the rings. Then repeat the process once again, a two-dip process in each bowl for each of the rings.

5. Immediately fry rings in the hot oil for about 4 to 5 minutes.

6. Briefly drain rings on paper towels before serving.

7. Repeat steps 4 through 6 for remaining onion rings.

John Bostick
Cincinnati, Ohio

SURE-FIRE POTATOES

Total Servings: 4–6
Preparation Time: 30 minutes
Challenge Level: Easy

"Potatoes with lower starch and higher moisture content are best for pan-frying. These turn crispy on the outside while remaining moist and flavorful on the inside. Red-skinned potatoes and all new potatoes fit the bill. And potato skins? Sure, they're good for you, but this isn't the only reason for leaving them on in this recipe. When the sugar in the potato caramelizes, the skin turns crunchy, giving a very nice combination of textures."

Preparation at Camp:

1. Cut potatoes into ¾-inch bite-size cubes.

2. Warm oil in frying pan over medium heat, then add rosemary, garlic, salt, and potatoes.

3. Fry potatoes, stirring occasionally, until crispy on the outside and soft on the inside.

John Bostick
Cincinnati, Ohio

2 pounds skin-on red or new potatoes, washed

3 tablespoons extra-virgin olive oil

1 tablespoon minced fresh rosemary

2 cloves garlic, minced

Salt to taste

Required Equipment:
Large frying pan

MONTEREY RICE

Total Servings: 5–7
Preparation Time: 30 minutes
Challenge Level: Easy

V

2 tablespoons sunflower oil

1¹/₂ cups regular rice

2 cups tomato juice

2 cups water

1 teaspoon garlic salt

1 teaspoon ground cumin

Required Equipment:
Medium-size frying pan

Medium-size mixing bowl

Preparation at Camp:

1. Warm oil in a frying pan over medium heat.

2. Brown rice in the pan, being careful not to burn it. Remove pan from the heat.

3. Combine tomato juice, water, garlic salt, and cumin in a bowl and mix well.

4. Return pan to low heat and add tomato juice mixture to the rice.

5. Cook slowly, covered and without stirring, for about 20 minutes, until rice is light and fluffy.

Vikki Voorhees Condrey
Columbus, Georgia

CANDIED LEMON CARROTS

V-LO

Total Servings: 2–3
Preparation Time: 15 minutes
Challenge Level: Easy

Preparation at Camp:

1. In a pot, cook carrots in a small amount of boiling water.

2. Drain carrots and transfer to a bowl.

3. Melt butter in the same pot over low heat, then stir in sugar.

4. Remove pot from heat, then stir in lemon juice.

5. Add carrots to pot, toss, then serve.

1 pound carrots, peeled and sliced into bite-size pieces

¼ cup (½ standard stick) butter

¼ cup granulated sugar

1 teaspoon lemon juice

Required Equipment:
Medium-size cook pot

Small bowl

Debra Moore
Sutton, Massachusetts

STEAMED BLUEBERRY ASPARAGUS

Total Servings: 3–4
Preparation Time: 15 minutes
Challenge Level: Easy

V

Water as per step 1 instructions

1 bunch fresh asparagus, trimmed and rinsed

¼ cup blueberry vinegar

Optional: salt to taste

Required Equipment:
Cook pot large enough to hold small cake rack

Small round or square cake rack

Preparation at Camp:

1. Place cake rack in the bottom of a pot. Add enough water to reach just the rack but no higher.

2. Set asparagus directly on top of rack.

3. Steam over high heat for 6 to 8 minutes, until asparagus becomes just tender.

4. Drain water, remove rack, retaining asparagus in pot.

5. Sprinkle asparagus with blueberry vinegar. Toss and serve hot with optional salt to taste.

Glenn Larsen
Pocatello, Idaho

HAWAIIAN MACARONI SALAD

Total Servings: 6–8
Preparation Time: 30 minutes
(plus about 1 hour to chill)
Challenge Level: Easy

V-LO

"Adapted from a recipe we found in Cook's Country, *this is the authentic macaroni salad I remember so fondly as a child growing up in Hawaii. It's great for picnics and goes well with nearly anything.* Ono *(delicious)!"*

—CHRISTINE

Preparation at Camp:

1. Cook macaroni according to package directions, but allow to boil a little longer than specified so pasta becomes very soft.

2. Drain pasta and pour into a medium-size bowl. Add vinegar to the pasta and toss.

3. In a small bowl, combine milk, mayonnaise, brown sugar, salt, and black pepper.

4. Stir the milk mixture well and pour over the pasta.

5. Add green onions, carrot, and celery to the pasta and toss.

6. Cover salad and chill in the cooler for about 1 hour before serving.

Christine and Tim Conners
Statesboro, Georgia

½ pound elbow macaroni

¼ cup cider vinegar

1 cup whole milk

1 cup mayonnaise

1½ teaspoons brown sugar

¼ teaspoon salt

1 teaspoon ground black pepper

2 green onions, thinly sliced

1 small carrot, peeled and finely grated

1 stalk celery, diced

Required Equipment:
Medium-size cook pot

Medium-size mixing bowl

Small mixing bowl

MOUNTAIN GOLD CORN

V-LO

Total Servings: 1
Preparation Time: 15 minutes
Challenge Level: Easy

1 ear sweet corn,
shucked

Butter to taste

Salt to taste

Granulated sugar to
taste

Grated Parmesan
cheese to taste

Preparation at Camp:

1. Place corn on a sheet of foil and top with butter, salt, sugar, and Parmesan cheese to taste.

2. Wrap corn loosely in foil, sealing edges tightly, then place on a grate over the coals, not in a direct flame.

3. Cook corn for about 15 minutes, rotating at least once while grilling.

Required Equipment:
Heavy-duty aluminum
foil

Hunter Hackworth
Pax, West Virginia

INDIAN CORN

Total Servings: 1
Preparation Time: 30 minutes
Challenge Level: Moderate

V

Preparation at Camp:

1. Peel back corn husk without tearing it off, then remove corn silks.

2. Pull the husk back up to completely cover the kernels.

3. Set corn in a bowl or container filled with water to soak for at least 15 minutes.

4. Place ear of corn, with husk still covering the kernels, directly on low embers in the campfire.

5. Cook corn for 10 minutes, rotating occasionally. Keep a close eye on the husk to be sure it doesn't catch fire.

6. Carefully remove corn from the campfire and serve with optional butter and salt.

1 ear corn, with husk

Optional: butter, salt to taste

Required Equipment:
Large bowl

> Avoid placing the corn in a very hot area of the campfire. It may burn otherwise.

Millie Hutchison
Pittsburgh, Pennsylvania

MUD POTATOES

Total Servings: 1
Preparation Time: 1 hour
Challenge Level: Moderate

1 large baking potato, unpeeled

Optional: sour cream, chives, butter to taste

Required Equipment:
None

Preparation at Camp:

1. Completely encase potato in heavy clay mud about ½ inch thick.

2. Lay mud-covered potato directly in the hot coals of the campfire.

3. Bake for about an hour. The mud will protect the potato while baking.

4. Carefully remove potato from the coals, crack open the mud (which will have hardened), then serve potato with optional garnishes.

Clean mud may sound like an oxymoron, but only mud from a nonpolluted source is to be used for this recipe to avoid potentially transferring toxic chemicals into the potato. The extreme heat of the campfire will neutralize any microbial life originally present in the mud, so no worries there.

While soil is found everywhere, few locales will have the kind of mud ideal for this recipe. Avoid disturbing the forest floor or digging deeply for the perfect clay, and only use this recipe if you can follow low-impact camping principles.

Donna Pettigrew
Anderson, Indiana

POP ONION

V-LO

Total Servings: 1
Preparation Time: 1¼ hours
Challenge Level: Easy

Preparation at Camp:

1. Cook onion, with skin intact, directly on hot coals for about an hour.

2. Carefully remove onion from coals and allow to cool for about 10 minutes.

3. Slice an X into the top of the onion, then squeeze the insides of the onion onto a serving plate, discarding the charred exterior.

4. Top onion with butter and salt to taste, then serve.

1 large sweet onion

Butter to taste

Salt to taste

Required Equipment:
None

Delano LaGow
Oswego, Illinois

BACON-ONION BALLS

Total Servings: 1
Preparation Time: 1¼ hours
Challenge Level: Moderate

1 medium-size sweet
onion

2 strips bacon

1 tablespoon butter

Required Equipment:
Heavy-duty aluminum
foil

Preparation at Camp:

1. Slice off the ends of the onion and remove the outer skin.

2. Wrap bacon around the onion in a crisscross pattern.

3. Carefully wrap onion in foil, avoiding excessive bunching of the foil, which can cause uneven cooking.

4. Set wrapped onion directly in the coals and bake for about an hour, turning frequently, until bacon has fully cooked and onion is soft.

5. Slice onion into four large wedges, melt butter over the top, and serve.

Christine and Tim Conners
Statesboro, Georgia

POTATO KABOBS

Total Servings: 2–3
Preparation Time: 30 minutes
Challenge Level: Easy

Preparation at Camp:

1. Pour oil in a small bowl and the bread crumbs in another.

2. Roll each new potato first in the oil then in the bread crumbs.

3. Thread coated potatoes onto the skewers.

4. Place kabobs on a grate about 3 inches over the embers.

5. Grill for about 10 minutes, rotating occasionally, until potatoes are crisp and golden brown on the outside.

¼ cup olive oil

⅓ cup Italian-style bread crumbs

1 (15-ounce) can whole new potatoes, well drained

Required Equipment:
Metal skewers

2 small mixing bowls

Millie Hutchinson
Pittsburgh, Pennsylvania

Photo by John Burbidge

CHEF-OF-THE-WOODS SWEET POTATOES

V-LO

Total Servings: 2–3
Preparation Time: 45 minutes
Challenge Level: Moderate

"Another recipe that I learned from Alex Eaton, a real chef of the woods."

1 sweet onion, thinly sliced into discs

1 tablespoon brown sugar

Salt and ground black pepper to taste

1 medium-size sweet potato, peeled and thinly sliced

2 tablespoons maple syrup

2 tablespoons cold butter, thinly sliced

1 teaspoon dried thyme

Preparation at Camp:

1. Lay onion slices on a large sheet of foil.

2. Sprinkle onions with brown sugar, salt, and black pepper.

3. Lay sweet potato slices over the onions.

4. Drizzle maple syrup over the potatoes, then lay pats of butter over the syrup.

5. Sprinkle all with thyme.

6. Create a pouch around the potatoes, sealing foil tightly around the edges.

7. Place foil packet on a grate a few inches over campfire embers.

8. Grill for 30 to 40 minutes, until potatoes are tender.

Required Equipment:
Heavy-duty aluminum foil

Keith Huffstetler
Winston-Salem, North Carolina

BACKCOUNTRY BRUSCHETTA

Total Servings: 4
Preparation Time: 30 minutes
Challenge Level: Easy

Preparation at Camp:

1. Combine tomatoes, basil, and garlic in a small bowl.

2. Slice baguette loaf crosswise into two pieces, then liberally brush the top of each half with olive oil.

3. Wrap each baguette half in a foil pouch and seal edges tightly.

4. Place foil pouches on a grate over coals.

5. Bake for about 5 minutes, rotating occasionally, until bread is toasty.

6. Stir tomato mixture and spoon over bread before serving.

2 cups chopped fresh tomatoes

1/4 cup chopped fresh basil

1 tablespoon fresh minced garlic

1 loaf hard-crusted baguette

1/4 cup olive oil

Required Equipment:
Small mixing bowl

Heavy-duty aluminum foil

Beverly Jo Antonini
Morgantown, West Virginia

SPRINGER MOUNTAIN POTATOES

Total Servings: 4
Preparation Time: 45 minutes
Challenge Level: Easy

4 red potatoes, chopped into ¾-inch cubes

1 large Vidalia onion, cut into ½-inch wedges

2 tablespoons olive oil

2 tablespoons McCormick Grill Mates Roasted Garlic & Herb Seasoning

Required Equipment:
Medium-size mixing bowl

Heavy-duty aluminum foil

Preparation at Camp:

1. In a bowl, coat potatoes and onions in oil.

2. Place vegetables in the center of a large sheet of foil.

3. Sprinkle seasoning over the vegetables.

4. Fold up corners of foil and seal tightly.

5. Place foil pack on a grate over the embers and grill for about 15 minutes on each side, until potatoes are tender.

Christine and Tim Conners
Statesboro, Georgia

MOUNTAIN GOAT GRILLED VEGGIES

V-LO

Total Servings: 6–8
Preparation Time: 30 minutes
Challenge Level: Easy

Preparation at Camp:

1. Combine mushrooms, onions, olive oil, Italian seasoning, salt, and black pepper in a bowl. Toss to mix.

2. Place vegetable mix in a greased grill basket and cook over embers or low flame for about 10 minutes, until onions soften.

3. Shake basket to mix veggies, then add tomatoes. Continue to cook for an additional 5 minutes.

4. Return cooked vegetables to the bowl and add goat cheese. Toss. Allow cheese to melt for a couple of minutes before serving.

Christine and Tim Conners
Statesboro, Georgia

1 pound fresh whole mushrooms, sliced in half

1 large red onion, sliced into 1/2-inch-thick disks

2 tablespoons olive oil

1 tablespoon Italian seasoning mix

1/2 teaspoon salt

1/2 teaspoon ground black pepper

1 pint grape tomatoes

4 ounces crumbled goat cheese

Required Equipment:
Medium-size mixing bowl

Grill basket

WILD ASPARAGUS AND GARLIC

Total Servings: 6–8
Preparation Time: 30 minutes
Challenge Level: Easy

V-LO

"Think of South Dakota, and what probably comes to mind is Mt. Rushmore, the Black Hills, or the infamous Corn Palace. But what many folks don't know about our state is that asparagus actually grows wild here! This recipe was created on the spot during a campout after we ran across some asparagus growing in a ditch."

2 bunches fresh asparagus, rinsed, trimmed, and chopped into 1-inch pieces

8 cloves garlic, minced

1 teaspoon dried dill weed

6 tablespoons (¾ standard stick) cold salted butter

Optional: ½ cup shredded Parmesan cheese

Required Equipment:
Heavy-duty aluminum foil

Preparation at Camp:

1. Lay asparagus pieces in a single layer on a large sheet of foil.

2. Sprinkle minced garlic and dill weed over the asparagus.

3. Slice butter into pats and distribute over the asparagus.

4. Tightly seal the foil, maintaining a thin layer of asparagus while doing so.

5. Place foil pack on a preheated grill. Cover grill and cook at medium heat for about 15 minutes.

6. Carefully open foil to avoid steam burns, then sprinkle with optional Parmesan cheese before serving.

Rob Venenga
Canton, South Dakota

RAINWATER CRACKER SALAD

V-LO

Total Servings: 4–6
Preparation Time: 15 minutes
Challenge Level: Easy

Preparation at Camp:
1. Combine all ingredients in a bowl. Stir well.

2. Serve immediately, before crackers completely soften.

Boil plenty of eggs at home before leaving for camp, enough for recipes such as this but also for eating as a side or snack.

1 (4-ounce) sleeve saltine crackers, coarsely crushed

1 medium tomato, diced

1 onion, diced

3 eggs, boiled and diced

1 cup mayonnaise

Required Equipment:
Medium-size mixing bowl

Robert Rainwater
Brookwood, Alabama

Breads

Photo by Scott Simerly

CAMP BISCUITS

Total Servings: 2 per cup of dough mixture
Preparation Time: 45 minutes
Challenge Level: Moderate

V-LO

"This is a from-scratch biscuit mix recipe, less expensive than the refrigerated type."

Preparation at Camp:

1. Combine all dry ingredients in a bowl and stir well.

2. Slowly add oil to the bowl while mixing.

3. Knead dough until oil is well blended throughout the flour. About 5 cups dough mixture will be produced. Use as much of the dough as needed, and store the remainder in a ziplock bag or container in a cooler.

4. Use 1/4 cup cold water per 1 cup dough mixture, kneading well and adding more water in very small amounts if mix seems overly dry.

5. Roll or form dough into a 1/2-inch-thick sheet, then cut biscuits from the sheet using an empty, clean can as a cutter.

6. Arrange biscuit dough rounds flat on the bottom of a Dutch oven, close together. Place the lid on the oven.

7. Bake for 20 to 30 minutes using 13 coals on the lid and 6 under the oven, until biscuit tops turn a light brown. Rotate oven frequently while cooking to prevent biscuit bottoms from burning.

Option: *Dough can also be used to make dumplings.*

Katie Salyer Cox
Tucson, Arizona

4 cups all-purpose flour

2/3 cup instant dry nonfat milk

1 teaspoon salt

3 tablespoons baking powder

1/2 cup olive oil

1/4 cup cold water per 1 cup dough mixture

Required Equipment:
Large mixing bowl

10-inch camp Dutch oven

Small, empty, clean can for cutting dough

DOUGH PUNCHER'S BISCUITS

V-LO

Total Servings: 3–4
Preparation Time: 45 minutes
Challenge Level: Easy

"Not much of a camp cook? Here is an easy recipe to make everyone think you are!"

2 tablespoons butter

1 teaspoon garlic salt

1 (12-ounce) package refrigerated biscuits

Required Equipment:
10-inch camp Dutch oven

Preparation at Camp:

1. In a Dutch oven over 21 coals, melt butter and stir in the garlic salt.

2. While butter is melting, split each biscuit in half and loosely roll dough into a ball.

3. Set dough balls in the hot butter and gently toss and roll until the dough is just beginning to brown on the surface.

4. Place lid on the oven and transfer 14 coals from under the oven to the lid.

5. Bake for about 15 minutes, until biscuits become fluffy and golden brown.

Options: *Try adding dried onions, dried herbs, or Parmesan cheese to the butter before browning the dough balls.*

Christine and Tim Conners
Statesboro, Georgia

GRAMMAW'S CORN BREAD

Total Servings: 6–8
Preparation Time: 45 minutes
Challenge Level: Easy

Preparation at Camp:

1. Mix all ingredients together in a bowl.

2. Pour batter into a Dutch oven.

3. Using 14 coals on the lid and 7 under the oven, bake for about 30 minutes, until corn bread is golden brown.

Pamela Jurgens-Toepke
New Lenox, Illinois

1 (8.5-ounce) package Jiffy corn muffin mix

1 (8-ounce) can whole corn, drained

1 (8-ounce) can cream-style corn

1/2 cup (1 standard stick) butter, softened

2 eggs

1/2 cup granulated sugar

Required Equipment:
Medium-size mixing bowl

10-inch camp Dutch oven

MEXICAN CORN BREAD

Total Servings: 8–10
Preparation Time: 1¹/₄ hours
Challenge Level: Moderate

2 (8.5-ounces) packages
Jiffy Corn Muffin Mix

1 cup milk

1 (15-ounce) can corn,
drained

1 cup diced onion

1 cup shredded cheddar
cheese

1 jalapeño pepper, diced

Required Equipment:
Medium-size mixing
bowl

10-inch camp Dutch
oven

Preparation at Camp:

1. Combine all ingredients in a bowl. Mix well.

2. Pour corn bread batter into a Dutch oven. Place lid on the oven.

3. Using 16 coals on the lid and 7 under the oven, bake for about 50 minutes, until a knife inserted into the corn bread comes out clean.

Be sure to occasionally reposition the oven over the coals while baking to prevent hot spots and charring.

Martha Charles
Rock Hill, South Carolina

INDIAN FRY BREAD

Total Servings: 4
Preparation Time: 30 minutes
Challenge Level: Easy

V

Preparation at Camp:

1. Combine 1 cup flour, seasonings, and water in a bowl. Mix well.

2. Warm oil over medium heat in a frying pan.

3. With floured hands, create 4 dough balls of roughly equal size, place in pan, and flatten with a spatula.

4. Fry on both sides until golden brown.

Christine and Tim Conners
Statesboro, Georgia

1 cup self-rising flour plus a little extra for working the dough

1 teaspoon Italian seasoning blend

½ teaspoon garlic salt

½ cup water

3 tablespoons olive oil

Required Equipment:

Small mixing bowl

Medium-size frying pan

Spatula

CORN BREAD IN AN ORANGE

Total Servings: 4
Preparation Time: 30 minutes
Challenge Level: Easy

"The orange skins provide natural bowls for the baked muffins and impart a citrus flavor to the corn cake."

4 medium-size oranges

1 (8.5-ounce) package Jiffy corn muffin mix

1 egg

1 teaspoon sugar

⅓ cup milk

Required Equipment:
Small mixing bowl

Heavy-duty aluminum foil

Preparation at Camp:

1. Slice oranges in half and remove pulp, being careful not to tear the skin. The pulp isn't required for this recipe, so eat the pieces now or save them for later.

2. In a bowl, combine corn muffin mix, egg, sugar, and milk.

3. Fill each orange half with corn muffin mixture, dividing it equally among the 8 pieces.

4. Realign the orange halves into 4 spheres, then wrap each sphere in foil.

5. Place foil spheres directly on hot coals. Heat for 8 to 10 minutes, until corn muffin mix has fully cooked.

Hollowed orange halves can be used to cook many of your favorite bread, muffin, or cake mixes.

Beth Ann Ast
Michigan City, Indiana

PEACE PIPE GARLIC BREAD

V-LO

Total Servings: 4–6
Preparation Time: 15 minutes
Challenge Level: Easy

Preparation at Camp:
1. Cut bread diagonally into 1-inch-thick slices but *do not* cut all the way through the loaf. The loaf should remain connected, end to end.

2. In a bowl, combine butter, garlic powder, and cheese. Mix well.

3. Spread butter mixture in between each slice of bread.

4. Wrap loaf completely in foil and place on grate over campfire embers but not in direct flame.

5. Cook for about 10 minutes, rotating often, until bread is warmed through.

1 (1-pound) loaf French bread

½ cup (1 standard stick) butter, softened

1 teaspoon garlic powder

¼ cup grated Parmesan cheese

Required Equipment:
Small mixing bowl

Heavy-duty aluminum foil

Jeanie Hass
Redwood Falls, Minnesota

THYME FOR GARLIC BREAD!

Total Servings: 4–6
Preparation Time: 30 minutes
Challenge Level: Easy

4 cloves garlic, minced

3 tablespoons olive oil

2 teaspoons dried thyme

2 teaspoons dried parsley

³/₄ teaspoons dried marjoram

Optional: ¼ cup fresh grated Parmesan cheese

1 (1-pound) loaf French bread

Required Equipment:
Small mixing bowl

Heavy-duty aluminum foil

Preparation at Camp:

1. Combine garlic, oil, thyme, parsley, marjoram, and optional Parmesan cheese in a bowl. Mix well.

2. Cut bread diagonally into 1-inch-thick slices but *do not* cut all the way through the loaf. The loaf should remain connected, end-to-end.

3. Drizzle oil-seasoning blend into each cut in the loaf.

4. Wrap loaf completely in foil and place on a grill over medium heat.

5. Cook for about 20 minutes, rotating occasionally, until bread is warmed through.

Christine and Tim Conners
Statesboro, Georgia

Snacks and Desserts

AUSTIN APPLES

Total Servings: 4
Preparation Time: 45 minutes
Challenge Level: Easy

4 Granny Smith apples, cored

4 regular-size marshmallows

¼ cup cinnamon red hot candies

Required Equipment:
Heavy-duty aluminum foil

8-inch camp Dutch oven

Preparation at Camp:

1. Stuff a marshmallow into the bottom of each of the cored apples.

2. Divide cinnamon candies among the 4 apples, filling the cores over the stuffed marshmallows.

3. Wrap each apple in foil.

4. Set wrapped apples upright in a Dutch oven. Place the lid on the oven.

5. Using 10 coals on the lid and 5 under the oven, bake for about 25 minutes, until apples are soft and steamy.

Gerry Garges
Austin, Texas

CAMP CUSTARD

Total Servings: 4
Preparation Time: 1¼ hours
Challenge Level: Easy

V-LO

Preparation at Camp:

1. Combine all ingredients, except for the optional caramel topping, in a bowl. Stir well to blend.

2. Grease insides of 4 heatproof mugs or cups.

3. Evenly divide custard among the mugs.

4. Set 10-inch pie pan on a trivet in a Dutch oven.

5. Place mugs on pie pan and fill pan with water. Place lid on the oven.

6. Using 21 coals on the lid and 11 under the oven, bake for about 50 minutes, until custard begins to pull away from the sides of the mugs. Refresh coals as needed.

7. Carefully remove mugs and serve with optional caramel topping.

½ (1-pound) loaf white bread, torn into small pieces

1¼ cups milk

1 teaspoon vanilla extract

½ teaspoon ground cinnamon

1 cup granulated sugar

1 tablespoon butter, softened

2 eggs, beaten

Optional: caramel topping

Required Equipment:
Medium-size mixing bowl

4 heatproof mugs or cups

Deep 14-inch camp Dutch oven with trivet

10-inch round aluminum pie pan

This is the only recipe in this book that calls for this oven size. Unless cooking for a large crowd, you rarely need such a behemoth. However, large sizes do provide additional options for creative cooking due to the voluminous interior, as this recipe illustrates.

Mary Young
Sunset, Louisiana

VANILLA APPLE CRISP

Total Servings: 4–6
Preparation Time: 1 hour
Challenge Level: Easy

V-LO

½ cup firmly packed brown sugar, divided

2 teaspoons ground cinnamon, divided

½ teaspoon vanilla extract

4 large Granny Smith apples, cored and thinly sliced

¼ cup honey

⅓ cup regular oatmeal

¼ cup (½ standard stick) unsalted butter, softened

25 vanilla wafers, crushed

Optional: whipped cream to taste

Required Equipment:
Medium-size mixing bowl

10-inch camp Dutch oven

Preparation at Camp:

1. Combine ¼ cup brown sugar, 1 teaspoon cinnamon, vanilla extract, and apples together in a bowl.

2. Stir to coat the apples, then pour into a Dutch oven.

3. Drizzle honey over apples in the oven.

4. Combine oatmeal, ¼ cup brown sugar, and 1 teaspoon cinnamon in the previously used bowl. Stir in the butter and crushed wafers. Mix well.

5. Evenly spread wafer mixture over the apples. Place lid on the oven.

6. Using 14 coals on the lid and 7 under the oven, bake for about 30 minutes, until the apples are tender.

7. Serve with optional whipped cream.

Jason Cagle
Jacksonville, Florida

CHOCOLATE LAVA CAKE

Total Servings: 5–7
Preparation Time: 1¹/₄ hours
Challenge Level: Easy

V-LO

Preparation at Camp:

1. Prepare cake batter by combining sugar, cocoa powder, flour, baking powder, and salt in a medium-size bowl.

2. Blend milk, butter, and vanilla extract into the flour mixture.

3. Line a Dutch oven with greased aluminum foil. Pour cake batter into the prepared oven.

4. Prepare topping by combining sugar and cocoa powder in a small bowl.

5. Sprinkle topping mix over batter in the oven.

6. Cover topping mix with water. Do not stir! Place lid on the oven.

7. Using 11 coals on the lid and 5 under the oven, bake for 40 to 50 minutes, until batter turns firm.

8. Serve with optional whipped topping.

Debra Moore
Sutton, Massachusetts

Cake:
³/₄ cup granulated sugar

3 tablespoons cocoa powder

1 cup all-purpose flour

2 teaspoons baking powder

¹/₄ teaspoon salt

¹/₂ cup milk

5 tablespoons butter, softened

1¹/₂ teaspoons vanilla extract

Topping:
¹/₂ cup granulated sugar

¹/₄ cup cocoa powder

1¹/₄ cups water

Optional: whipped cream

Required Equipment:
Medium-size mixing bowl

8-inch camp Dutch oven

Heavy-duty aluminum foil

Small mixing bowl

CRYSTAL RIVER CHERRY COBBLER

Total Servings: 6–8
Preparation Time: 1 hour
Challenge Level: Easy

V-LO

1 (21-ounce) can cherry pie filling

1 (18.25-ounce) package yellow or white cake mix

¼ cup (½ standard stick) cold butter

¼ cup milk

Required Equipment:
10-inch camp Dutch oven

Heavy-duty aluminum foil

Preparation at Camp:

1. Pour pie filling into a Dutch oven lined with greased foil.

2. Sprinkle dry cake mix evenly over the pie filling.

3. Slice butter into pats and distribute over the cake mix.

4. Pour milk over all. Do not stir! Place lid on the oven.

5. Using 14 coals on the lid and 7 under the oven, bake for 40 to 50 minutes, until cobbler begins to brown.

Shawn Desjardins
Fort Lauderdale, Florida

TINKER MOUNTAIN PUMPKIN TREAT

Total Servings: 6–8
Preparation Time: 1¼ hours
Challenge Level: Easy

V-LO

"The Appalachian Trail crosses Tinker Mountain. It's a special place for my family."

Preparation at Camp:

1. Combine all ingredients, except for the optional whipped cream, in a bowl. Thoroughly mix.

2. Pour batter into a Dutch oven. Place lid on the oven.

3. Using 14 coals on the lid and 7 under the oven, bake for about 1 hour, until dough becomes firm. Refresh coals as needed.

4. Serve with optional whipped cream.

Do not confuse pure pumpkin with pumpkin filling. The latter will not work well with this recipe.

Craig Depuy
Clemmons, North Carolina

1 (15-ounce) can pure pumpkin

1 (12-ounce) can evaporated milk

1 cup granulated sugar

1 teaspoon vanilla extract

½ teaspoon ground cinnamon

1 (15.25-ounce) package yellow cake mix

½ cup (1 standard stick) butter, softened

Optional: whipped cream to taste

Required Equipment:
Medium-size mixing bowl

10-inch camp Dutch oven

TEMPTATION TORTE

Total Servings: 6–8
Preparation Time: 1¼ hours
Challenge Level: Easy

V-LO

½ cup (1 standard stick) butter, softened

1 cup all-purpose flour

½ cup pecan meal

8 ounces cream cheese

1 cup confectioners' sugar

1 (8-ounce) container Cool Whip whipped topping

1 pound fresh berries, such as blueberries, raspberries, or sliced strawberries

Required Equipment:
Small mixing bowl

Heavy-duty aluminum foil

10-inch camp Dutch oven

Medium-size mixing bowl

Preparation at Camp:

1. Combine butter, flour, and pecan meal in a small bowl. Mix well.

2. Press pecan mixture into the bottom of a Dutch oven lined with greased foil. Place lid on oven.

3. Using 14 coals on the lid and 7 under the oven, bake crust for about 15 minutes, then set aside to cool.

4. Once crust cools, blend cream cheese, sugar, and Cool Whip in a medium-size bowl.

5. Spread cream cheese blend evenly over cooled crust.

6. Cover cream cheese blend with fruit, then serve.

Donna Pettigrew
Anderson, Indiana

184

AWARD-WINNING APPLE-CRANBERRY COBBLER

Total Servings: 8–10
Preparation Time: 1 hour
Challenge Level: Easy

V-LO

"I prepared a version of this recipe a number of years ago for a Scoutmaster's Cook-Off and won!"

Preparation at Camp:

1. Combine apple pie filling and cranberry sauce in a Dutch oven and stir.

2. Pour 1 cup chopped walnuts evenly over fruit.

3. Separate cinnamon roll dough into individual pieces, then slice each roll into two disks.

4. Distribute roll disks evenly over the fruit and nuts.

5. Sprinkle the second cup of chopped nuts over the rolls. Place lid on the oven.

6. Using 16 coals on the lid and 7 under the oven, bake for 30 to 40 minutes, until rolls are a golden brown.

7. Drizzle icing from dough container over rolls and serve.

1 (21-ounce) can apple pie filling

1 (14-ounce) can whole-berry cranberry sauce

2 cups chopped walnuts, divided

1 (12.4-ounce) container Pillsbury refrigerated cinnamon rolls with icing

Required Equipment:
10-inch camp Dutch oven

Mike Russell
Harker Heights, Texas

PINEAPPLE UPSIDE-DOWN CAKE

Total Servings: 8–10
Preparation Time: 1 hour
Challenge Level: Moderate

V-LO

1 (15.25-ounce) can pineapple slices, undrained

1 (8-ounce) can crushed pineapple, undrained

½ cup (1 standard stick) cold butter

1 cup brown sugar

1 (10-ounce) jar maraschino cherries, drained

1 (15.25-ounce) package Pillsbury traditional yellow cake mix

3 eggs

⅓ cup sunflower oil

Required Equipment:
10-inch camp Dutch oven

Heavy-duty aluminum foil

Medium-size mixing bowl

Heatproof serving plate

Preparation at Camp:

1. Reserve 1 cup pineapple juice from the pineapple slices and crushed pineapple. Drain the remainder of the juice.

2. Slice butter into thin pats and arrange in the bottom of a foil-lined Dutch oven.

3. Evenly sprinkle brown sugar over the butter.

4. Set pineapple rings over the brown sugar, covering the bottom, side-by-side, no more than a single-layer deep.

5. Place cherries in holes in the pineapple rings and in the gaps between the pineapple slices.

6. In a bowl, combine cake mix, eggs, oil, drained crushed pineapple, and the cup of pineapple juice previously set aside. Mix well to remove lumps.

7. Place Dutch oven over 21 coals and allow butter to melt.

8. Place lid on oven, then transfer 14 coals to the lid, leaving 7 under the oven.

9. Bake for 30 to 40 minutes, until top of cake is golden brown and an inserted knife comes out clean.

10. Remove lid, and using heavy oven mitts, carefully place a heatproof serving plate upside down over the oven. Carefully flip the oven to drop cake onto the plate. The foil will remain attached to the cake as it drops.

11. Remove foil from the cake and serve.

Mike "Mountain Man Mike" Lancaster
Clovis, California

RED HOT COBBLER

V-LO

Total Servings: 8–10
Preparation Time: 1¼ hours
Challenge Level: Easy

"This cobbler is always an eye-opener during my Dutch oven cooking demos thanks to its colorful presentation."

Preparation at Camp:

1. Drain the syrup from 2 cans of peaches into a bowl. Add cake mix to the bowl and stir well to blend.

2. Pour juice from the third can of peaches into a foil-lined Dutch oven and spread all the peaches in the juice.

3. Sprinkle half the package of cinnamon candies over the peaches.

4. Pour cake batter over peaches then sprinkle the remainder of the cinnamon candies over the batter. Place lid on the oven.

5. Using 14 coals on the lid and 7 under the oven, bake for about 1 hour, refreshing coals as needed. Cobbler is ready to serve once top becomes golden brown.

3 (15.25-ounce) cans sliced peaches in heavy syrup

1 (18.25-ounce) package yellow or white cake mix

1 (6-ounce) package cinnamon red hot candies

Required Equipment:
Medium-size mixing bowl

Heavy-duty aluminum foil

10-inch camp Dutch oven

Mike Russell
Harker Heights, Texas

BACKWOODS BAKLAVA

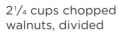

Total Servings: 8–10
Preparation Time: 1¼ hours
Challenge Level: Difficult

V-LO

2¼ cups chopped walnuts, divided

¼ cup brown sugar

1 tablespoon ground cinnamon

1 (16-ounce) package Athens Fillo Dough twin-pack 9 x 14-inch sheets

1 cup (2 standard sticks) butter, melted

½ cup honey

¼ cup granulated sugar

2 tablespoons water

Required Equipment:
Small mixing bowl

10-inch camp Dutch oven

Heavy-duty aluminum foil

Small cook pot

Preparation at Camp:

1. Combine 2 cups chopped walnuts, brown sugar, and cinnamon in a bowl.

2. Unroll fillo sheets and cut in half, producing 4 sets of sheets, each about 9 x 7 inches in size. Keep fillo sheets covered with a slightly damp cloth while working, as the sheets will otherwise dry out.

3. Line a Dutch oven with foil and brush bottom with melted butter.

4. Using about a third of the fillo dough, arrange sheets in an overlapping pinwheel style to cover bottom of oven, gently brushing each set of pieces with butter as you go.

5. Evenly spread about half the walnut-sugar-cinnamon mixture over the dough.

6. Repeat steps 4 and 5.

7. Add the remainder of fillo dough in pinwheel style, again brushing with butter.

8. Sprinkle ¼ cup chopped walnuts over the top of the dough.

9. Using a sharp knife, gently slice a lattice pattern through the top layer of dough. Place lid on the oven.

10. Using 14 coals on the lid and 7 under the oven, bake for about 50 minutes, until top of dough becomes golden brown. Refresh coals if needed.

11. While baklava bakes, prepare syrup by combining honey, granulated sugar, and water in a small pot then simmer over low heat.

12. Once baklava has finished baking, pour syrup over top. The syrup will run into the cracks of the dough and soak into the layers.

13. Allow baklava to cool for a few minutes before serving.

Laurie Hatch
West Linn, Oregon

NONNA'S SUNDAY CAKE

Total Servings: 8–10
Preparation Time: 2½ hours
Challenge Level: Moderate

V-LO

Cake:
3 eggs, beaten

1 (8-ounce) can crushed pineapple

2 teaspoons vanilla extract

5 bananas, mashed

1 cup sunflower oil

1 teaspoon ground cinnamon

1 (18.25-ounce) package yellow cake mix

Optional: 1½ cups chopped walnuts

Icing:
¼ cup (½ standard stick) butter, softened

4 cups confectioners' sugar

1 (8-ounce) can crushed pineapple

Required Equipment:
Large mixing bowl

10-inch camp Dutch oven

Heavy-duty aluminum foil

Medium-size mixing bowl

Preparation at Camp:
1. Combine cake ingredients in a large bowl, adding and mixing in one ingredient at a time in the order listed.

2. Pour cake batter into a Dutch oven lined with greased foil. Place lid on the oven.

3. Bake the cake using 14 coals on the lid and 7 under the oven for 60 to 70 minutes, until an inserted knife comes out clean. Refresh coals as needed.

4. With Dutch oven off the coals, remove lid and allow cake to cool completely.

5. While cake cools, combine all icing ingredients in a medium-size bowl and stir well.

6. Flip oven over to drop the cake onto a serving plate, then spread icing over cake before serving.

Beverly Jo Antonini
Morgantown, West Virginia

TWIGS

V-LO

Total Servings: 3–5
Preparation Time: 1 hour
Challenge Level: Easy

Preparation at Camp:

1. Melt peanut butter and butterscotch morsels together in a pot over low heat.

2. Once sauce is smooth, stir in the noodles.

3. Drop coated noodles by the teaspoonful onto waxed paper.

4. Chill in the cooler or evening air to solidify before serving.

$^2/_3$ cup peanut butter

1 cup butterscotch morsels

1 (3-ounce) can chow mein noodles

Required Equipment:
Small cook pot

Waxed paper

You can substitute lightly greased aluminum foil for the waxed paper.

George Brown
Los Osos, California

STAR GAZER'S POPCORN

Total Servings: 4
Preparation Time: 15 minutes
Challenge Level: Moderate

V-LO

"Instead of eating popcorn at the movies, kick back in a camp chair at night, look up, and enjoy your popcorn while watching the universe!"

1 tablespoon olive oil

¼ cup (½ standard stick) cold butter

1 cup popping corn

Salt to taste

Required Equipment:
Large cook pot, at least 12-inches deep

Preparation at Camp:

1. Pour oil in a pot. Swirl oil around to entirely coat the bottom.

2. Cut butter into slices and add to the pot.

3. Pour popping corn into the pot.

4. Cover pot and set over medium heat.

5. Shake pot often to move the kernels around so they don't burn.

6. Once popping slows to once every few seconds, remove corn from heat, then serve with salt to taste.

When cooking popcorn, don't wait until the popping stops completely. Otherwise the corn will have already badly burned. With practice, you'll learn to master the fine art of balancing unpopped corn with the occasional scorched kernel.

Harold Robinson
Quarryville, Pennsylvania

BLACKBERRY CRISP

Total Servings: 5–7
Preparation Time: 15 minutes
Challenge Level: Easy

V

"A quick crisp for camping!"

Preparation at Camp:

1. Pour pie filling in a pot, then warm over low heat until thin.

2. Once filling begins to bubble gently, pour granola into the pot. Stir.

3. Cover pot and allow to simmer for 5 minutes before serving.

1 (21-ounce) can Comstock Premium Blackberry Filling

1 cup crisp granola cereal

Required Equipment:
Medium-size cook pot

Option: You can substitute your favorite pie filling flavor for the blackberry.

> Granola comes in an array of types and styles, some of which are uncooked, while others are baked and packaged for use as cereal with milk. The latter tends to be crispy and is the kind you want to use with this recipe.

Leslie Anderson
Harrison, Arkansas

PINE CONES

Total Servings: 1
Preparation Time: 15 minutes
Challenge Level: Easy

Water as per step 1 instructions

1 teaspoon chocolate syrup

1 teaspoon topping: shredded coconut, Rice Krispies, chopped nuts, or sprinkles

1 regular-size marshmallow

Required Equipment:
3 small bowls

Camping fork

Preparation at Camp:
1. Place 3 bowls on your work surface: the first containing a small amount of water, the second containing the chocolate syrup, and the third containing the topping of your choice.

2. Quickly dip marshmallow in the bowl of water. The water will help prevent the marshmallow from flaming while over the campfire.

3. Place the marshmallow on a camping fork and toast over the campfire until golden brown.

4. Immediately roll hot marshmallow in chocolate syrup, followed by a dip in the bowl of topping.

Option: If no campfire is available for roasting the marshmallows, uncooked marshmallows can be rolled in melted chocolate or icing before dipping in the topping.

Millie Hutchison
Pittsburgh, Pennsylvania

PEACHES AND SUNSHINE

Total Servings: 1
Preparation Time: 15 minutes
Challenge Level: Easy

Preparation at Camp:

1. Place peach half on a small square of foil, with the pit hole facing upward.

2. Add brown sugar to the pit hole, then top with a marshmallow.

3. Wrap foil around the peach and seal, leaving a little room in the pouch.

4. Set foil on a grate over coals for 5 to 10 minutes, until marshmallow melts.

½ peach from a can

1 teaspoon brown sugar

1 regular-size marshmallow

Required Equipment:
Heavy-duty aluminum foil

Donna Pettigrew
Anderson, Indiana

CLIFF HANGER'S CHERRY DELIGHT

V-LO

Total Servings: 1
Preparation Time: 15 minutes
Challenge Level: Easy

2 (³/₄-inch-thick) slices pound cake

2 tablespoons cherry pie filling

Whipped cream to taste

Required Equipment:
Pie iron

Preparation at Camp:
1. Place a slice of cake in each side of a well-greased pie iron.

2. Spread cherry pie filling on one of the slices of cake.

3. Close pie iron and set over the embers of the campfire.

4. Cook for about 10 minutes, turning occasionally.

5. Serve with whipped cream.

> Actual pie-iron cooking times will vary depending on the proximity of the iron to the fire, the temperature of the coals, the type of pie iron used, and whether the iron has been preheated.

Margaret Bushman
Waterford, Michigan

WICKED-GOOD HOT BANANAS

Total Servings: 1
Preparation Time: 15 minutes
Challenge Level: Easy

"Yes, they are bananas. Yes, they are hot. And, yes, they are really wicked good!"

Preparation at Camp:

1. With peel on, slice banana partially through along the length of the inside curve.

2. Gently squeeze banana to open cavity.

3. Pack banana with cream cheese, chocolate chips, peanut butter morsels, mini marshmallows, and optional fruit.

4. Wrap banana in foil and set on grate over coals.

5. Cook banana for 3 to 5 minutes per side.

6. Remove foil packet from the grate. Carefully unwrap, then serve.

1 banana

1 tablespoon cream cheese

1 tablespoon chocolate chips

1 tablespoon peanut butter morsels

1 tablespoon mini marshmallows

Optional: wild fruit like huckleberries, blueberries, or blackberries, if available

Laura Sell
Freeport, Florida

Required Equipment:
Heavy-duty aluminum foil

MEXICAN S'MORES

Total Servings: 1
Preparation Time: 15 minutes
Challenge Level: Easy

1 (10-inch) flour tortilla

3 tablespoons mini marshmallows

3 tablespoons mini chocolate chips

Optional: Nutella, honey, peanut butter, chopped nuts, chopped Snickers bar, Heath English Toffee Bits

Required Equipment:
Heavy-duty aluminum foil

Preparation at Camp:

1. Set tortilla on a sheet of foil.

2. Place all ingredients, including any optional ingredients, on the tortilla and roll like a burrito.

3. Wrap foil securely around tortilla.

4. On a grate over coals, warm the foil packet for about 5 minutes before serving.

Michael Zopes
Thornton, Colorado

Photo by Scott Simerly

CARAMEL S'MORES

Total Servings: 1
Preparation Time: 15 minutes
Challenge Level: Moderate

Preparation at Camp:

1. Thread marshmallow onto a camping fork. Follow the marshmallow with a cube of caramel.

2. Roast the marshmallow and caramel over a bed of coals, not a flaming fire.

3. Once marshmallow is golden, not burned, pull it up over the caramel so that the caramel is inside the marshmallow. Be careful, because the caramel will be hot.

4. Allow to cool for a few minutes, then serve with a piece of chocolate and graham cracker.

1 regular-size marshmallow

1 cube caramel candy

1 small piece of chocolate

1 small graham cracker

Required Equipment:
Camping fork

Jeanie Hass
Redwood Falls, Minnesota

BANANA BOATS

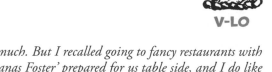

V-LO

Total Servings: 1
Preparation Time: 15 minutes
Challenge Level: Moderate

"Frankly, I don't like bananas very much. But I recalled going to fancy restaurants with my mom and dad and having 'Bananas Foster' prepared for us table side, and I do like bananas served that way. So I grabbed a little brown sugar, butter, cinnamon, and orange juice and gave it a try. It made for a very yummy, warm, and gooey treat!"

1 banana

1 tablespoon brown sugar

½ tablespoon cold butter, thinly sliced

1 dash ground cinnamon

1 tablespoon orange juice

Optional toppings: chopped nuts, whipped cream, Simple Squishy Ice Cream (see recipe later in this chapter)

Required Equipment:
Heavy-duty aluminum foil

Preparation at Camp:

1. With peel on, slice banana partially through along the length of the inside curve.

2. Slice again, parallel but at an angle to the first cut, to form a notch cut along the length of the banana.

3. Pull peel aside and remove banana meat from the notch and eat it. A V-shaped cavity should be left behind in the banana.

4. Spoon brown sugar into the cavity, then lay pats of butter over the sugar.

5. Sprinkle cavity with cinnamon, then dribble orange juice over the cinnamon.

6. Spoon optional nuts into the cavity.

7. Replace banana peel over cavity and double wrap the banana in foil.

8. Lay foil pack directly on campfire embers, cavity side up.

9. Cook for about 5 minutes, carefully remove foil pack from the embers, and open.

10. Serve straight from the foil pack with optional whipped cream or ice cream.

Laurie Hatch
West Linn, Oregon

CAMPFIRE UPSIDE-DOWN CAKES

V-LO

Total Servings: 4
Preparation Time: 15 minutes
Challenge Level: Easy

Preparation at Camp:

1. On each shortcake, layer 1 tablespoon butter, 1 tablespoon brown sugar, 1 pineapple ring, and 1 cherry.

2. Lay a square of foil over the top of the shortcake stack and flip the entire cake upside down onto the foil.

3. Seal the foil packet and place on a grate over coals, pineapple side down, and bake for about 10 minutes before serving.

Donna Pettigrew
Anderson, Indiana

4 ready-made single-serving shortcakes

¼ cup (4 tablespoons) butter

¼ cup (4 tablespoons) brown sugar

4 pineapple rings from a can

4 maraschino cherries

Required Equipment:
Heavy-duty aluminum foil

Photo by John Burbidge

INSIDE-OUT CARAMEL APPLES

V-LO

Total Servings: 4
Preparation Time: 30 minutes
Challenge Level: Easy

4 large baking apples

½ cup cinnamon red hot candies

4 cubes caramel

Required Equipment:
Heavy-duty aluminum foil

Preparation at Camp:

1. Core the apples, leaving a small amount of apple at the bottom of each so that the candies won't fall through.

2. Fill each cored apple with 2 tablespoons cinnamon candies.

3. Place caramel cube in the top of each apple, molding it to create a seal.

4. Wrap each apple in two layers of foil, with enough foil left over at the top of each to create a handle to make it easier to extract the apples from the embers.

5. Place apples directly on coals for about 15 minutes, turning occasionally, until apple can be easily pierced with a fork.

6. Carefully remove apples from fire and allow to cool before serving.

> Pippin or Granny Smith apples work well with this recipe.

Blennie Danielson
Arcadia, California

CANNONBALLS

V-LO

Total Servings: 4
Preparation Time: 30 minutes
Challenge Level: Easy

Preparation at Camp:

1. Combine brown sugar, raisins, nuts, and cinnamon in a bowl. Mix well.

2. Core the apples, leaving the bottom on the apples to retain juices.

3. Place apples on individual sheets of foil. Spoon sugar mixture into the cored centers of each apple.

4. Set a piece of butter into the top of the mixture in each apple.

5. Double-wrap each apple tightly in foil.

6. Place apples upright on coals and cook until tender, about 15 minutes.

7. Allow apples to cool slightly before serving.

Robert Rainwater
Brookwood, Alabama

¼ cup light-brown sugar

¼ cup raisins

2 tablespoons chopped pecans or walnuts

½ teaspoon ground cinnamon

4 large Granny Smith apples

2 tablespoons cold butter, cut into 4 pieces

Required Equipment:
Small mixing bowl

Heavy-duty aluminum foil

DONUT-ON-A-STICK

V-LO

Total Servings: 5
Preparation Time: 30 minutes
Challenge Level: Easy

"Everyone loves this one!"

½ cup (1 standard stick) butter, softened

1 tablespoon ground cinnamon

¼ cup granulated sugar

1 (12-ounce, 10-count) container refrigerated biscuit dough

Required Equipment:
Metal cup

Small mixing bowl

Camping forks

Preparation at Camp:

1. Melt butter in metal cup over gentle heat.

2. Combine cinnamon and sugar in a bowl and stir.

3. Break each refrigerated biscuit into thirds, then roll each piece into a ball.

4. Thread dough balls onto camping forks, several on each.

5. Cook dough balls over the coals, rotating often until dough is fully cooked.

6. Dip baked dough balls in the melted butter.

7. Immediately roll buttered dough balls in the sugar-cinnamon mixture, then serve.

Donna Pettigrew
Anderson, Indiana

LITTLE ANGELS

V-LO

Total Servings: 5–7
Preparation Time: 15 minutes
Challenge Level: Easy

Preparation at Camp:

1. Cut cake into 2-inch cubes.

2. Open can of condensed milk and discard lid.

3. Pour coconut flakes in a heap on a plate.

4. Slide a piece of cake onto a camping fork and dip in the condensed milk.

5. Roll soaked cake in coconut flakes.

6. Roast cake over the fire for a few minutes until heated through.

1 (10-ounce) loaf angel food cake

1 (14-ounce) can sweetened condensed milk

1 (7-ounce) package sweetened flaked coconut

Required Equipment:
Camping forks

Option: You can substitute pound cake for the angel food cake.

Judy Gratsch
Grand Blanc, Michigan

ECLIPSE APPLE PIE

V-LO

Total Servings: 8
Preparation Time: 30 minutes
Challenge Level: Moderate

"I prepared this recipe for the first time while camping with my family on Flint Ridge. We ate our dessert in the freezing cold while watching a lunar eclipse!"

1 (15-ounce) package of 2 refrigerated piecrusts

1 (21-ounce) can apple pie filing

1 cup brown sugar

1/2 cup granulated sugar

1/4 cup (1/2 standard stick) cold butter

Required Equipment:
Heavy-duty aluminum foil

Preparation at Camp:

1. Slice each piecrust in half to make a total of 4 pastry dough pieces.

2. Place each piece of pastry dough on a separate sheet of foil. Each sheet of foil should be at least twice the size of the pastry dough once pastry is folded in half.

3. Evenly divide pie filling among the centers of the 4 pastry dough pieces.

4. Divide brown and granulated sugars among the 4 pies, leaving enough sugar for sprinkling the outsides of the pies in step 6.

5. Fold each piece of pastry dough over the filling. Close by pinching the edges shut. If crust is reluctant to adhere, wet inside edges with water and pinch again.

6. Place a pat of butter on both sides of each pie, then sprinkle each side with remaining sugars.

7. Fold foil over, centering the pie in the pocket. Tightly seal foil by folding edges 3 times over. Leave a little room within the foil packet around the pie.

8. Place foil packs on a grate over embers and cook for about 10 minutes per side.

9. Carefully remove baked pies from foil packs and split each to create 8 servings total.

Option: You can substitute other pie fillings for the apple.

Kimra Simmons
Abingdon, Maryland

MOCK APPLE PIE

Total Servings: 8
Preparation Time: 1 hour
Challenge Level: Easy

V-LO

"I created this recipe by mistake while on a camping trip in Iowa. As always, I packed the food. But on this particular trip, I accidently brought apple filling instead of beans. Voilà!"

Preparation at Camp:

1. Lightly butter only one side of each slice of bread.

2. Load a slice of bread into the pie iron, buttered side against the iron.

3. Spread several heaping tablespoons of pie filling over the slice of bread.

4. Cover filling with a second slice of buttered bread, buttered side up.

5. Close pie iron and hold over a campfire for about 5 to 10 minutes, occasionally rotating, until filling is warmed through and bread begins to toast.

4 tablespoons butter, softened

1 (1-pound) loaf white bread

1 (21-ounce) can apple pie filling

Required Equipment:
Pie iron

Option: You can substitute your favorite pie filling for the apple.

Use more than one pie iron to speed the cooking process.

*LeeAnn Kercheval
Antioch, Illinois*

STRAWBERRY LONG CAKES

V-LO

Total Servings: 1
Preparation Time: Less than 5 minutes
Challenge Level: Easy

"I adapted this recipe from a version I saw on the Food Channel *during a special on baseball park cuisine. A form of this dessert was being sold by vendors at a Class-A baseball park in the Midwest."*

¼ cup fresh or frozen strawberries or blueberries

1 Little Debbie Cloud Cake

⅓ cup Cool Whip whipped topping

Preparation at Camp:
1. Thaw fruit if using frozen.
2. Break Cloud Cake into large pieces and place in a drinking cup.
3. Spoon fruit over cake, then top with Cool Whip.

Required Equipment:
None

> The original recipe called for a Twinkie instead of a Cloud Cake. That was before Hostess filed for bankruptcy and the seemingly immortal Twinkie was heading toward an uncertain future. Should the Twinkie resurrect, by all means, use it!

Vince Wahler
Albuquerque, New Mexico

SIMPLE SQUISHY ICE CREAM

V-LO

Total Servings: 1
Preparation Time: 30 minutes
Challenge Level: Easy

Preparation at Camp:

1. Combine milk, sugar, and vanilla extract in a quart-size ziplock bag. Seal tightly, expelling as much air as possible while doing so.

2. Fill a gallon-size ziplock bag half full with crushed ice, then add rock salt.

3. Slide quart-size bag into the ice in the gallon size bag. Seal gallon-size bag tightly.

4. Gently massage bag of ice around the milk bag for about 15 minutes, until the ice cream freezes.

Option: A popular variation to this recipe is called "kick-the-can" ice cream. Instead of using freezer bags, the milk mix is placed in a small coffee can, which is then placed in a larger coffee can filled with ice and rock salt. Both cans are sealed tightly with duct tape. The kids then kick the can around for about 15 minutes, until the ice cream freezes.

Laurie Hatch
West Linn, Oregon

1 cup whole milk

2 tablespoons granulated sugar

½ teaspoon vanilla extract

Required Equipment:
Quart-size ziplock freezer bag

Gallon-size ziplock freezer bag

Crushed ice

6 tablespoons rock salt

EARTH WORM PUDDING

V-LO

Total Servings: 4
Preparation Time: 15 minutes
Challenge Level: Easy

1 (3.4-ounce) package
instant chocolate
pudding mix

1 cup cold milk

10 Oreo cookies,
crushed

1 (5-ounce) package
gummy worms

Required Equipment:
Quart-size ziplock bag

4 mugs or bowls

Preparation at Camp:

1. Pour pudding mix and milk into a quart-size ziplock bag.

2. Seal bag and shake well to mix. Allow bag to rest a few moments while pudding sets.

3. Add crushed Oreos and gummy worms to the bag. Knead gently until cookies and gummy worms are mixed.

4. Divide pudding among 4 mugs or bowls and serve.

Millie Hutchison
Pittsburgh, Pennsylvania

BANANA PUDDING PIE

V-LO

Total Servings: 4
Preparation Time: 15 minutes
Challenge Level: Easy

Preparation at Camp:

1. Combine pudding mix with milk in a quart-size ziplock bag.

2. Seal bag and shake well to mix. Let rest for a few minutes to set.

3. Evenly layer crushed cookies in 4 mugs or bowls.

4. Top cookies with banana slices.

5. Snip a corner from the bottom of the pudding bag and squeeze contents over the banana slices, dividing pudding evenly among the 4 servings.

1 (3.4-ounce) package instant banana cream pudding mix

1 cup cold milk

20 vanilla wafer cookies, crushed

2 bananas, sliced

Required Equipment:
Quart-size ziplock bag

4 mugs or bowls

Donna Pettigrew
Anderson, Indiana

FUDGE-IN-A-BAG

V-LO

Total Servings: 6–8
Preparation Time: 15 minutes
Challenge Level: Easy

"I invented this fudge recipe while living in Kuwait. At the time, I was making no-cook frosting and had the thought that it could be altered a bit to make fudge while camping, sort of like 'pudding in a bag.'"

½ cup cocoa powder

4½ cups confectioners' sugar

½ cup (1 standard stick) butter

1 teaspoon vanilla extract

4 ounces cream cheese

Required Equipment:
Gallon-size ziplock freezer bag

Preparation at Camp:

1. Combine all ingredients in a large ziplock bag. Squeeze out as much air as possible, then seal bag tightly.

2. Knead contents until all ingredients are well mixed.

3. Lay bag on a table, flatten the fudge in the bag to an even depth, then slit the sides of the bag to expose the fudge.

4. Cut fudge into pieces, then serve.

> This recipe may not work well when the weather is very hot and the butter wants to melt, or when it's very cold and the butter and cream cheese remain stiff.

Katie Salyer Cox
Tucson, Arizona

ADIRONDACK MOUNTAIN CLUB GORP

Total Servings: 8
Preparation Time: Less than 5 minutes
Challenge Level: Easy

V-LO

"This recipe was awarded 'Best Tasting Gorp' in a contest sponsored by the Genesee Valley Chapter of the Adirondack Mountain Club."

Preparation at Camp:

1. Combine all ingredients in a bowl. Toss to mix.

2. Divide gorp among 8 pint-size ziplock bags for snacking in camp or when hiking and exploring.

Option: *Try adding walnuts for a burst of flavor.*

Avoid carrying the gorp in a very hot pack, because the Reese's Pieces may melt.

Larry Reister
Rochester, New York

1 pound roasted peanuts

1 pound raisins

1 (12.6-ounce) package plain M&Ms

1 (10-ounce) package Reese's Pieces

Required Equipment:
Large mixing bowl

8 pint-size ziplock bags

HIKIN' S'MORES

Total Servings: 8–10
Preparation Time: Less than 5 minutes
Challenge Level: Easy

1 (13-ounce) package
Golden Grahams cereal

1 (10.5-ounce) package
mini marshmallows

1 (19.2-ounce) package
plain M&Ms

Required Equipment:
Medium-size mixing
bowl

8–10 snack-size ziplock
bags

Preparation at Camp:

1. Combine all ingredients in a bowl. Toss.

2. Pack in 8 to 10 snack-size ziplock bags for hiking or snacking around camp.

Christine and Tim Conners
Statesboro, Georgia

S'MORES PDQ

Total Servings: 8–10
Preparation Time: Less than 5 minutes
Challenge Level: Easy

"I came up with this idea when I needed an easy and fun no-cook dessert for about six hundred campers!"

Preparation at Camp:

1. Pour chocolate and peanut butter chips into a large aluminum tray or pan. Shake to mix.

2. Spread an 1/8-inch-thick layer of marshmallow crème over 2 graham cracker planks.

3. Press the first graham cracker plank, marshmallow crème side down, into the chips.

4. Place the second plank, crème side down, onto the chip-laden plank, then serve.

1 (12-ounce) package chocolate chips

1 (10-ounce) package peanut butter chips

1 (7-ounce) jar marshmallow crème

1 (14.4-ounce) package graham crackers

Required Equipment:
Large aluminum tray or pan

Option: You can substitute M&Ms for the chocolate chips and Reese's Pieces for the peanut butter chips.

Gerry Garges
Austin, Texas

S'MORES PIE

Total Servings: 8–10
Preparation Time: 1¼ hours
Challenge Level: Moderate

3 cups mini marshmallows, divided

2 cups semisweet chocolate chips, divided

⅓ cup milk

2 cups cold heavy whipping cream

1 (9-ounce) package Keebler Ready Crust Graham 2 Extra Servings piecrust

Required Equipment:
2 medium-size mixing bowls

Small cook pot

Whisk

Preparation at Camp:

1. Chill a mixing bowl in a cooler.

2. While mixing bowl chills, combine 1 cup marshmallows, 1¾ cups chocolate chips, and milk in cook pot and warm over low heat. Stir until marshmallows are melted.

3. Pour chocolate-marshmallow mixture into a second bowl, then cool to "room" temperature.

4. Add cold whipping cream to the chilled bowl. Whisk cream until stiff peaks form. This can take several minutes.

5. Fold 3 cups of whipped cream and 2 cups marshmallows into the now-cool chocolate mixture.

6. Spoon whipped cream–chocolate mixture into the piecrust.

7. Sprinkle ¼ cup chocolate chips onto pie and cover with remaining whipped cream.

8. Chill pie for about 15 minutes in the cooler before serving.

Roger Brow
Bowie, Maryland

Drinks

CANDY BAR COCOA

Total Servings: 1
Preparation Time: 15 minutes
Challenge Level: Easy

V-LO

1 single-serving candy
bar: Snickers, Milky Way,
Twix, York Peppermint
Patty, or Hershey's

1 cup milk

1 single-serving packet
instant hot cocoa mix

Required Equipment:
Small cook pot

Preparation at Camp:

1. Chop candy bar into pieces.

2. Bring milk to a low boil in a pot.

3. Pour hot milk into a mug.

4. Add cocoa mix and candy bar pieces to the hot milk.

5. Stir until candy bar pieces have begun to melt, then serve.

Christine and Tim Conners
Statesboro, Georgia

CLIMBER'S CHOCO-LATTE

V-LO

Total Servings: 1
Preparation Time: 15 minutes
Challenge Level: Easy

"Whether you've just come down from a hard climb, or spent the day in the tent, this recipe is sure to make you smile."

Preparation at Camp:

1. Warm milk in a pot. Do not bring to a boil.

2. Add instant coffee, sugar, and cocoa powder to the warm milk.

3. Stir well and serve.

Christine and Tim Conners
Statesboro, Georgia

1 cup milk

1 heaping teaspoon instant coffee

2 tablespoons granulated sugar

2 tablespoons cocoa powder

Required Equipment:
Small cook pot

GINGER TEA

Total Servings: 1
Preparation Time: 15 minutes
Challenge Level: Easy

V

"A wonderfully spicy tea with a host of medicinal benefits."

1 cup water

Fresh ginger root

1 teaspoon honey

Required Equipment:
Small cook pot

Preparation at Camp:

1. Bring water to a boil in a pot, then pour into a mug.

2. Immediately peel ginger root and shred about 5 (1-inch) slivers into the mug.

3. Allow root to steep for about 10 minutes.

4. Add honey, stir, then serve with or without ginger slivers remaining in the mug.

Option: *On a hot day serve tea over ice.*

Christine and Tim Conners
Statesboro, Georgia

FRESH MINT TEA

Total Servings: 1
Preparation Time: 15 minutes
Challenge Level: Easy

V

Preparation at Camp:

1. Bring water to a boil in a pot, then pour into a mug.

2. Add mint leaves to the mug and allow to steep for about 10 minutes.

3. Add honey, stir, then serve with or without leaves remaining in the mug.

Option: On a hot day serve tea over ice.

Christine and Tim Conners
Statesboro, Georgia

1 cup water

12 fresh mint leaves

1 teaspoon honey

Required Equipment:
Small cook pot

BOOT STOMPIN' JELL-O JUICE

Total Servings: 2
Preparation Time: 15 minutes
Challenge Level: Easy

"A little decadent, but a lot of fun."

2 cups water

1 (3-ounce) package Jell-O gelatin (your choice)

Required Equipment:
Small cook pot

Preparation at Camp:
1. Bring water to a boil in a pot, then divide between 2 mugs.

2. Evenly divide Jell-O mix between the mugs.

3. Stir and serve.

Christine and Tim Conners
Statesboro, Georgia

COWBOY COFFEE

Total Servings: 12 (about 6 ounces each)
Preparation Time: 15 minutes
Challenge Level: Easy

V

"Our friend, Pete Fish, taught us how to make cowboy coffee on the trail. We've dabbled with his original recipe over the years to adapt it to camp. We've found cowboy coffee to be remarkably resilient against variations in cooking. Even when it's overboiled, it's still pretty darn good. Once, we inadvertently left an open pot of coffee over a low, smoky campfire for about a half hour. It was still at a moderate boil when we rediscovered it. Figuring it would be a bitter mess, instead it was the best camp coffee we've ever tasted: smooth and mellow, presumably from the smoke."

Preparation at Camp:

1. Over cold water in a pot, float coffee grounds to form a thick mat.

2. Bring water to a boil momentarily, then remove pot from heat.

3. Add a splash of cold water to settle any grounds that remain floating on the surface.

4. Carefully scoop coffee from the top of the liquid to avoid disturbing the settled grounds, unless you like your coffee chewy.

1 cup coffee grounds, medium grind

3 quarts cold water

Required Equipment:
Medium-size cook pot

Options: Experiment with different grinds, roasts, strengths, beans, and boiling times to find your perfect cup of camp coffee. And don't forget to try a little mellowing in the campfire smoke.

Christine and Tim Conners
Statesboro, Georgia

RASPBERRY MINT MILK

V-LO

Total Servings: 1
Preparation Time: Less than 5 minutes
Challenge Level: Easy

1 cup cold milk

2 tablespoons York Dark Chocolate & Peppermint Sundae Syrup

¼ teaspoon raspberry extract

Required Equipment:
None

Preparation at Camp:

1. Combine milk, syrup, and raspberry extract in a drinking cup.

2. Stir well and serve.

Option: You can also warm this drink in a pot and serve it hot.

Donna Pettigrew
Anderson, Indiana

RANGER RICK'S ORANGE CRUSH

V-LO

Total Servings: 8
Preparation Time: Less than 5 minutes
Challenge Level: Easy

Preparation at Camp:

1. Combine Jell-O and Tang in a pint-size ziplock bag. Shake to mix.

2. Add about 3 tablespoons drink mix to 1 cup cold milk in a drinking cup.

3. Stir well and serve.

Richard "Ranger Rick" Halbert
Traverse City, Michigan

1 (3.4-ounce) package French vanilla-flavored Jell-O Instant Pudding and Pie Filling

½ cup Tang Orange Drink Mix

1 cup cold milk per serving

Required Equipment:
Pint-size ziplock bag

LAZY DAZE LEMONADE

V

Total Servings: 8
Preparation Time: 15 minutes
Challenge Level: Easy

6 large lemons,
squeezed

1 cup granulated sugar

2 quarts water

Preparation at Camp:
1. Combine fresh lemon juice, sugar, and water in a pitcher.

2. Stir well and serve over ice.

Required Equipment:
2-quart pitcher

Maria Conners
Statesboro, Georgia

RASPBERRY SUNSHINE TEA

Total Servings: 8
Preparation Time: All day
Challenge Level: Easy

"I still can see that jar of sunshine tea, glistening on our picnic table from morning until the sun went down."

Preparation at Camp:

1. Early in the day, place tea bags in a container filled with water. Seal tightly.

2. Set container where it will be in direct sunlight for most of the day.

3. By suppertime, tea will be ready to serve over ice, garnished with fresh raspberries. Add optional sugar to taste.

Option: *Instead of the raspberry tea, try apple cinnamon–flavored tea garnished with a cinnamon stick, or lemon tea garnished with wedges of lemon.*

8 raspberry-flavored herbal tea bags

2 quarts water

1 pint fresh raspberries

Optional: granulated sugar to taste

Required Equipment:
2-quart clear container with lid

Kathleen Kirby
Milltown, New Jersey

TANGY TEA

Total Servings: 12
Preparation Time: Less than 5 minutes
Challenge Level: Easy

"Great either as a cool beverage by the lake or a hot drink by the campfire."

¾ cup Tang Orange
Drink Mix

½ cup granulated sugar

¼ cup instant
unsweetened tea mix

1 teaspoon ground
cinnamon

1 cup water per serving

Required Equipment:
Pint-size ziplock bag

Preparation at Camp:
1. Combine all dry ingredients in a pint-size ziplock bag. Shake to mix.

2. Add about 2 tablespoons drink mix to 1 cup water, cold or hot.

3. Stir well and serve.

Donna Pettigrew
Anderson, Indiana

APPENDIX A: COMMON MEASUREMENT CONVERSIONS

United States Volumetric Conversions

1 smidgen	1/32 teaspoon
1 pinch	1/16 teaspoon
1 dash	1/8 teaspoon
3 teaspoons	1 tablespoon
48 teaspoons	1 cup
2 tablespoons	1/8 cup
4 tablespoons	1/4 cup
5 tablespoons + 1 teaspoon	1/3 cup
8 tablespoons	1/2 cup
12 tablespoons	3/4 cup
16 tablespoons	1 cup
1 ounce	2 tablespoons
4 ounces	1/2 cup
8 ounces	1 cup
5/8 cup	1/2 cup + 2 tablespoons
7/8 cup	3/4 cup + 2 tablespoons
2 cups	1 pint
2 pints	1 quart
1 quart	4 cups
4 quarts	1 gallon
1 gallon	128 ounces

Note: Dry and fluid volumes are equivalent for teaspoon, tablespoon, and cup.

International Metric System Conversions
Volume and Weight

United States	Metric
1/4 teaspoon	1.25 milliliters
1/2 teaspoon	2.50 milliliters
3/4 teaspoon	3.75 milliliters
1 teaspoon	5 milliliters
1 tablespoon	15 milliliters

1 ounce (volume)	30 milliliters
¼ cup	60 milliliters
½ cup	120 milliliters
¾ cup	180 milliliters
1 cup	240 milliliters
1 pint	0.48 liter
1 quart	0.95 liter
1 gallon	3.79 liters
1 ounce (weight)	28 grams
1 pound	0.45 kilogram

Temperature

°F	°C
175	80
200	95
225	105
250	120
275	135
300	150
325	165
350	175
375	190
400	205
425	220
450	230
475	245
500	260

British, Canadian, and Australian Conversions

1 teaspoon . . . . approx. 1 teaspoon
(Britain, Canada, Australia)   (United States)

1 tablespoon . . . . approx. 1 tablespoon
(Britain, Canada)   (United States)

1 tablespoon . . . . 1.35 tablespoons
(Australia)   (United States)

1 ounce . . . . 0.96 ounce
(Britain, Canada, Australia)   (United States)

1 gill . . . . 5 ounces
  (Britain)   (Britain, Canada, Australia)

1 cup . . . . 10 ounces
  (Britain)   (Britain, Canada, Australia)

1 cup . . . . 9.61 ounces
  (Britain)   (United States)

1 cup . . . . 1.20 cups
  (Britain)   (United States)

1 cup . . . . 8.45 ounces
  (Canada, Australia)   (United States)

1 cup . . . . 1.06 cups
  (Canada, Australia)   (United States)

1 pint . . . . 20 ounces
  (Britain, Canada, Australia)   (Britain, Canada, Australia)

1 Imperial gallon . . . . 1.20 gallons
  (Britain)   (United States)

1 pound . . . . 1 pound
  (Britain, Canada, Australia)   (United States)

Equivalent Measures*

16 ounces water. . . . . 1 pound
2 cups vegetable oil . . . . 1 pound
2 cups or 4 sticks butter. . . . . 1 pound
2 cups granulated sugar. . . . . 1 pound
3½ to 4 cups unsifted confectioners' sugar . . 1 pound
2¼ cups packed brown sugar . . . . 1 pound
4 cups sifted flour. . . . . 1 pound
3½ cups unsifted whole wheat flour . . . . . 1 pound
8–10 egg whites. . . . . 1 cup
12–14 egg yolks. . . . . 1 cup
1 whole lemon, squeezed . . . . 3 tablespoons juice
1 whole orange, squeezed . . . . ⅓ cup juice

* Approximate

APPENDIX B: SOURCES OF EQUIPMENT AND SUPPLIES

Amazon
www.amazon.com
It's well-known that Amazon sells an enormous array of products. But it might come as a surprise nevertheless that it also hosts a very large number of vendors who sell exotic food ingredients difficult to find in your local grocery store. Check out Amazon if you're stumped when trying to find an ingredient.

Bass Pro Shops
www.basspro.com
Bass Pro stocks a large line of kitchen gear perfect for car camping, including a wide array of Lodge Dutch ovens and accessories. Bass Pro stores are a good place to go to see the equipment firsthand before you buy.

Bulk Foods
www.bulkfoods.com
Here you'll find an enormous selection of dried fruits, spices, grains, and nuts sold in a variety of sizes and quantities.

Cabela's
www.cabelas.com
This retailer specializes as a hunting and fishing outfitter but also carries a wide selection of outdoor kitchen gear and cookware. Cabela's has dozens of large retail stores located throughout the United States and Southern Canada.

Camp Chef
www.campchef.com
Many cast-iron cookware accessories are available through Camp Chef. The company also markets its own line of aluminum and cast-iron Dutch ovens, frying pans, and other cookware.

Campmor

www.campmor.com

Campmor stocks a huge selection of general camping supplies, many of them valuable for rounding out your list of basic equipment for a remotely located camp kitchen, farther from the car, where lightweight and compact are important characteristics for your gear.

Cascade Designs, Inc.

www.cascadedesigns.com

One of the most respected outdoor equipment manufacturers in the world, Cascade Designs' major brands include MSR stoves and cookware, Therm-a-Rest sleep gear, and Platypus hydration systems.

Chuck Wagon Supply

www.chuckwagonsupply.com

The range of cast-iron cookware and accessories at Chuck Wagon is truly impressive. This is a great site to compare different Dutch oven makes and models and to discover all those items you didn't know you needed. If you are looking for lighter weight aluminum ovens, you'll find a nice selection here. Chuck Wagon also stocks items of value for large groups, including, for instance, giant griddles, enormous coffee pots, and the like.

Costco

www.costco.com

This popular membership warehouse stocks serving ware in package sizes perfect for large groups. Retail stores are located throughout North America.

Dutch Oven Gear

www.dutchovengear.com

Sami Dahdal is CEO of Sam's Iron Works and its sister company, Dutch Oven Gear. A master wrought-iron craftsman, Sam manufactures quality tables and accessories for camp Dutch ovens. Check the website to see his gear in action.

Lodge Manufacturing

www.lodgemfg.com

Founded in 1896, Lodge is the premier source of a large array of high-quality cast-iron cookware and related accessories. It is the only company that still manufactures its full line of camp cast-iron cookware in the United States.

MACA Supply

www.macaovens.com

MACA manufactures a wide range of very deep camp cast-iron Dutch ovens, including what must be the largest on the market: a monster sporting a lid 22 inches in diameter and weighing in at 160 pounds! MACA also offers oval-shaped ovens, useful for roasting birds and larger cuts of meat.

REI

www.rei.com

Like Campmor, REI carries a large array of gear useful for the remote camp kitchen. REI also stocks an assortment of cast-iron cookware and accessories by Lodge.

Sam's Club

www.samsclub.com

Sam's Club, like Costco, is a large membership warehouse. Sam's has hundreds of retail locations across the United States and stocks a wide range of serving ware, kitchen supplies, and groceries in bulk package sizes.

Sport Chalet

www.sportchalet.com

Sport Chalet is a major outdoor recreation retailer in the southwest United States. Like Bass Pro Shops, this is a good place to go to see camp kitchen gear, Lodge cast iron, and related accessories before making the purchase.

The Wok Shop

www.wokshop.com

You'll find a great selection of high-quality, rugged Asian cookware appropriate for the camp environment at the Wok Shop's online retail store.

APPENDIX C: ADDITIONAL READING AND RESOURCES

Books and Periodicals
Chuck Wagon Supply Bookstore
www.chuckwagonsupply.com
This Dutch oven specialty shop has a great selection of books and posts a wealth of helpful information for those new to cast-iron cooking.

Cook's Illustrated and *Cook's Country*
www.cooksillustrated.com and *www.cookscountry.com*
These outstanding periodicals from America's Test Kitchen turn common recipes into wonderful re-creations but with a minimum of effort. Along the way, the reader learns how and why the recipes work. *Cook's Illustrated* explores fewer dishes but in more detail than *Cook's Country*, its sister publication, which comes in a larger format and full color. These are magazines for the home kitchen, but what you'll learn about indoor cooking will prove invaluable at camp.

Lodge Manufacturing Bookstore
www.lodgemfg.com
The preeminent manufacturer of camp cast-iron cookware, Lodge offers a wide range of books and DVDs that focus on recipes and cooking techniques at their factory outlet stores and on their website.

On Food and Cooking: The Science and Lore of the Kitchen
Harold McGee, Scribner
This is an excellent resource for understanding the science behind cooking. When chefs decipher why recipes work the way they do, they become much more effective at adapting recipes in a pinch or creating new ones on the fly. Be forewarned: This is not a cookbook, much less an outdoor cookbook. But if science interests you, this book will too.

The Scout's Dutch Oven Cookbook
Tim and Christine Conners, Globe Pequot Press
Focusing on the art of camp Dutch oven cooking, this book delves into technique without skimping on the recipes. Dozens of Dutch oven experts from throughout Boy Scouts of America contributed over one hundred outstanding and unique camp recipes.

The Scout's Large Groups Cookbook
Tim and Christine Conners, Globe Pequot Press
As with *The Scout's Dutch Oven Cookbook,* Boy Scout leaders spared none of their secrets in providing over one hundred excellent recipes, but in this case with a specific focus on groups of ten to twenty campers or more. A wide range of cooking methods and techniques is covered.

The Scout's Outdoor Cookbook
Tim and Christine Conners, Globe Pequot Press
The founding title of the Scout's Cookbook series, this book puts more emphasis on the recipes and less on the method. All popular forms of camp cooking are represented. Over three hundred recipes are included, many award winning, and all provided by Scout leaders from across the United States.

Informational Websites
Epicurious
www.epicurious.com
You won't find much on camp cooking at Epicurious, but if you're looking to hone your basic cooking skills and could use thousands of recipes for practice, this is a good resource.

Exploratorium
www.exploratorium.edu/cooking
Exploratorium makes cooking fun by putting emphasis on the science behind it. Even if you're not the scientist type, you'll enjoy this site. Quirky yet practical, recipes flow down the page with relevant science posted in the sidebar.

Gourmet Sleuth

www.gourmetsleuth.com

You can find a good kitchen measurement conversion calculator on this website. Included is a tool for converting between US and British measurement units.

International Dutch Oven Society (IDOS)

www.idos.com

The mission of IDOS is to preserve the art of Dutch oven cooking. According to IDOS, their organization is the largest and most productive group of "black pot" enthusiasts in the world.

Leave No Trace (LNT) Center for Outdoor Ethics

www.LNT.org

The Center for Outdoor Ethics has been a leader and respected voice in communicating why and how our outdoor places require responsible stewardship. The LNT outdoor ethics code is becoming standard practice in the wilderness. More information about the organization is available at their website, and specific information about outdoor ethics principles, especially as applied to cooking, can be found in Appendix D of this book.

APPENDIX D: LOW-IMPACT COOKING

The Leave No Trace Center for Outdoor Ethics provides a set of principles that are becoming increasingly well-known and applied by those who visit the wild places of the world.

These are the seven core principles of Leave No Trace:

- Plan ahead and prepare

- Travel and camp on durable surfaces

- Dispose of waste properly

- Leave what you find

- Minimize campfire impacts

- Respect wildlife

- Be considerate of other visitors

Careful planning, especially with respect to food preparation, is critical to successfully following the principles of Leave No Trace. When preparing for an upcoming outing, consider the following list of application points as you evaluate your food and cooking options.

Decide how you'll prepare your food.
Some methods of cooking, such as gas stoves and grills, create less impact than others, such as open fires. Low-impact principles are followed when using a camp Dutch oven with charcoal on a fire pan, provided the pan is placed on bare soil or rock, and the coal ash is disposed of in a discreet and fire-safe manner.

When using open fire to cook, follow local fire restrictions and use an established fire ring instead of creating a new one. Keep fires small. If wood gathering is permitted in your camping area, collect wood from the ground rather than from standing trees. To avoid creating barren earth, find wood farther away from camp. Select smaller pieces of wood, and burn them completely to ash. Afterward, be sure the fire is completely out. Don't bring firewood from home to camp if the wood might harbor insects or disease harmful to the flora in your camp area.

Carefully select and repackage your food to minimize trash.
Tiny pieces of trash easily become litter. Avoid bringing small, individu-ally packaged candies and other such food items. Twist ties and bread clips are easily lost when dropped. Remove the wrappers and repackage such foods into ziplock bags before leaving home; or use knots instead of ties and clips to seal bags and the like.

Metal containers and their lids, crushed beverage cans, and bro-ken glass can easily cut or puncture trash sacks. Wrap these carefully before placing them in thin-wall trash bags. Minimize the use of glass in camp. Scan your camp carefully when packing up to ensure that no litter is left behind.

Minimize leftovers and dispose of food waste properly.
Leftover foods make for messier trash and cleanup. If poured on open ground, they are unsightly and unsanitary. If buried, animals may dig them up. Leftovers encourage problem animals to come into camp if not properly managed. Carefully plan your meals to reduce leftovers. And if any remain, share with others or carefully repackage and set aside in a protected place to eat at a later meal.

Dispose of used wash and rinse water (also called gray water) in a manner appropriate for your camping area. Before disposal, remove or strain food chunks from the gray water and place these with the trash. If no dedicated gray water disposal area is available, scatter the water outside of camp in an area free of sensitive vegetation and at least two hundred feet from streams and lakes. Avoid creating too many suds by using only the amount of detergent necessary for the job. Bring only biodegradable soap to camp.

Plan to protect your food, trash, and other odorous items from animals.
Consider avoiding the use of very aromatic foods that can attract ani-mals. Store food, trash, and other odorous items where animals won't be able to get to them. Besides being potentially dangerous to the animal, and inconvenient for the camper, trash is often spread over a large area once the animal gains access. Follow local regulations regarding proper food storage.

Decide whether to avoid collecting wild foods.
Don't harvest wild foods, such as berries, if these are not plentiful in the area you're visiting. Such foods are likely to be a more important component of the local ecosystem when scarce.

These are only a few of the practical considerations and potential applications of the principles of Leave No Trace. Visit www.LNT.org for additional information and ideas.

INDEX

ABOUT THE AUTHORS

Experienced campers, backpackers, and outdoor chefs, Christine and Tim Conners are the authors of the nationally popular *Lipsmackin'* outdoor cookbook series, including the titles *Lipsmackin' Backpackin'*, *Lipsmackin' Vegetarian Backpackin'*, and, the latest entry to the series, *Lipsmackin' Car Campin'*.

Specifically for the Scouting world, Tim and Christine have produced the *Scout's Cookbook* series: *The Scout's Outdoor Cookbook*, *The Scout's Dutch Oven Cookbook*, *The Scout's Large Groups Cookbook*, and *The Scout's Backpacking Cookbook*. Each title in the *Scout's Cookbook* lineup is a collection of unique and outstanding recipes from Scout leaders across the United States.

Christine and Tim have been testing outdoor recipes for nearly twenty years. At the invitation of Boy Scouts of America, the Connerses have twice served as judges for *Scouting* magazine's prestigious national camp food cooking contest.

The Connerses have four children—James, Michael, Maria, and David—all of whom stay busy in the outdoors by backpacking on the Appalachian Trail, camping and day hiking in the local state parks, and kayaking on the region's lakes and rivers . . . when they aren't writing cookbooks!

Please visit us at www.lipsmackincampin.com, like us on Facebook at www.facebook.com/lipsmackincampin, or follow us on Twitter at www.twitter.com/lipsmackincampn.